Top Executive Compensation: 1988 Edition

by Elizabeth R. Arreglado
and Charles A. Peck

A Research Report from The Conference Board

Contents

Tables

COMMUNICATIONS

DIVERSIFIED SERVICE

ENERGY AND NATURAL RESOURCES

INSURANCE

LIFE INSURANCE

PROPERTY AND CASUALTY INSURANCE

TRADE

TRANSPORTATION

UTILITIES

Charts

Authors' Acknowledgment

Analytical programming was provided by Steven Gazis under the direction of E. Kay Worrell, Director, Records and Research Support. Charts were prepared under the direction of Chuck N. Tow, Chief Chartist.

From the President

The twenty-fifth edition of The Conference Board's report on top executive compensation appears at a time when the emphasis in U.S. industry is shifting from traditional manufacturing toward other types of business, particularly those in the service sector. To reflect the current play of forces in the U.S. economy, this year's report introduces material on compensation in communications, telecommunications, energy and natural resources, transportation, and wholesale trade. It also continues the coverage of diversified service firms begun in the 1987 edition and the Board's traditional in-depth treatment of compensation in the manufacturing, commercial banking, insurance, retail trade, and gas and electric utilities sectors.

The format of this year's report has been substantially revised to make it clearer and easier to use. For all industry sections, data are presented on the salary, bonus, and total current compensation paid to the five highest-paid executives. The opening chapter provides information on trends in total current compensation and base salary by industry category as well as projections of 1988 and 1989 budgets for salary increases.

The key forms of executive incentive compensation are analyzed in terms of prevalence, trends, and magnitude of compensation paid. These include annual bonus plans, restricted stock awards, long-term performance plans, and stock options. Because of the increasing importance of long-term performance plans, initial awards under these plans are analyzed for the first time.

Several hundred companies supplied data for the report. We thank them for contributing their time and effort to make this publication possible.

PRESTON TOWNLEY
President

Highlights

The 1987 compensation of the five highest-paid executives in each of 670 surveyed companies in nine major types of businesses is analyzed in this report. The major focus is on 1987 total current compensation defined as base salary paid in 1987 and bonus earned for 1987 company performance. Using this report, a company can compare the 1987 compensation of its top-paid executives with that of their counterparts in companies of similar size and type of business.

The report also describes the incidence of, and trends in, four important elements of the executive compensation package: annual bonus plans, long-term performance plans, stock option plans, and restricted stock plans. For stock options, the size of option grants during 1987 is shown, as well as the net gain for options exercised during 1987. For restricted stock plans, the size of grants during 1987 is reported. The size of payouts during 1987 is given for long-term performance plans. And, for the first time, the size of contingent awards made under these plans during the year is reported.

Pay Trends

Compared with 1986, 1987 total current compensation was higher in all the industry categories surveyed, except in transportation, where it was unchanged. Total current compensation increased 14.3 percent in diversified service, 11.1 percent in manufacturing, 10.4 percent in energy and natural resources, 9.2 percent in communications, 8.6 percent in utilities, 8.1 percent in insurance, 6.4 percent in trade, and 4.9 percent in commercial banking.

Salaries rose in 1987 in each type of business. The increase was 7.7 percent in communications, 7.3 percent in insurance, 7.2 percent in manufacturing, 7.0 percent in transportation, 6.6 percent in utilities, 6.5 percent in diversified service, 6.3 percent in commercial banking, 5.6 percent in trade, and 3.7 percent in energy and natural resources.

Estimates of salary increase budgets made in April and May 1988 for all salaried employees show a median increase of 4.8 percent for nonexempts, 5.0 percent for exempts, and 5.4 percent for executives for 1988. The projection for 1989 is the same for nonexempt and exempt salaried employees and is 5.3 percent for executives.

Annual Bonus Plans

The increased use of annual bonus plans continues among financial institutions: 89 percent of the surveyed commercial banks and insurance companies now have plans. Utilities have also continued to adopt bonus plans: 65 percent have plans. Annual bonuses are virtually universal in transportation, diversified service, manufacturing, and energy and natural resources. Eighty-eight percent of both communications and trade have plans.

The size of the median bonus award for the CEO, as a percentage of salary, is lowest in utilities and commercial banking, 31 and 37 percent, respectively. Insurance, trade, and communications show very similar patterns at 47 percent, 49 percent, and 50 percent, respectively. Energy companies paid a median bonus of 53 percent. Diversified service and transportation both had median CEO bonuses of 60 percent, while manufacturing was the high payer at 68 percent.

Restricted Stock Plans

Under these plans, companies make outright awards of restricted shares, which are often subject to forfeiture until "earned out" over a stipulated period of continued employment. A significant minority of companies in each type of business have a plan for awards of restricted stock to top executives: diversified service, 46 percent; energy, 42 percent; banks, 32 percent; manufacturing and trade, both 30 percent; stock insurance companies, 21 percent; transportation, 19 percent; communications, 12 percent; and utilities, 11 percent.

During 1987, the median award to the five highest-paid executives as a group ranged from a high of 54 percent of salary in the insurance industry to a low of 28 percent in utilities.

Long-Term Performance Plans

A minority of companies in each industry group have long-term performance plans. Top executives are given a contingent award of shares or units at the beginning of a performance period; the payment of these awards is determined by how closely specified corporate financial targets are met during a three-, four-, or five-year performance period. Such plans are most prevalent in energy, 39 percent; diversified service, 38 percent; and manufacturing, 35 percent. Twenty-nine percent of the surveyed communications companies have long-term performance plans, as do 24 percent of the banks, insurance companies, and utilities. Long-term plans are least often found in transportation (13 percent) and trade (12 percent).

During 1987, the median *award* to the five highest-paid executives as a group ranged from 60 percent of salary among manufacturers and energy and natural resources to 32 percent in utilities. The median *payment* for 1987 ranged from 44 percent of salary in banking to 19 percent in utilities.

Stock Option Plans

Generally, there has been some increase in the proportion of companies with stock option plans over the past few years: 94 percent of the surveyed communications companies have them; 84 percent of the energy companies; 83 percent of the manufacturers; 79 percent of both trade and diversified service; 70 percent of the banks; 69 percent of the transportation firms; 50 percent of the stock insurance companies; and 35 percent of the utilities.

The median stock option grant made in 1987 to the five highest-paid executives as a group ranged from the equivalent of 89 to 250 percent of base salary, depending on the type of business. The median net gain for options exercised during 1987 ranged from a high of 183 percent of salary in transportation firms to a low of 36 percent in utilities.

Method

Information for this report was collected during April and May 1988. Questionnaires were mailed to approximately 2,700 U.S. companies. Those surveyed were manufacturers with sales of $100 million or more and companies of comparable size in nine other industry categories.

Usable responses were received from 670 companies in nine industry categories. There was insufficient data for the tenth category, construction, to permit analysis. The 670 respondents were distributed by industry category as follows:

- Manufacturing companies (254)
- Gas, electric, water, and telephone utilities (111)
- Commercial banks (93)
- Life and property and casualty insurance companies (91)
- Wholesale and retail trade companies (33)
- Energy and natural resources companies (31)
- Diversified service companies, including computer services, health care, hotel/restaurant/entertainment, and real estate (24)
- Communications companies, including broadcasting and printing and publishing (17)
- Transportation companies (16)

Chapter 1
Introduction

This report is primarily an analysis of the 1987 compensation of the five highest-paid executives in each of 670 surveyed companies (see box on "Method"). The major emphasis is on base salary *paid* in 1987 and the bonus *earned* for 1987 company performance, regardless of when paid. Total current compensation is the sum of the two. The report also describes the prevalence of and trends in four major forms of executive incentive compensation: annual bonus plans, restricted stock plans, long-term performance plans, and stock option plans.

Pay Trends

The change in CEO total current compensation from 1986 to 1987 is given in Table 1 below. This is the median change for the position in those companies that furnished data in both years. The individuals in the CEO positions were not necessarily the same in both years. The same information with respect to salary is shown in Table 2.

As an indicator of future salary increases, companies were asked during April and May 1988 to provide the 1988 salary increase budget and the 1989 anticipated salary increase budget for their executive, exempt, and nonexempt populations. The results are shown in Table 3 for all industries as a group and separately for those industries for which the data were sufficient to allow individual analysis.

Table 1: CEO Total Current Compensation Change, 1987 over 1986

Industry Category	*Number of Companies*	*Median Change*
Diversified service	17	14.3%
Manufacturing	156	11.1
Energy and natural resources	15	10.4
Communications	9	9.2
Utilities	52	8.6
Insurance	48	8.1
Trade	19	6.4
Commercial banking	46	4.9
Transportation	8	0.0

Table 2: CEO Salary Change, 1987 over 1986

Industry Category	*Number of Companies*	*Median Change*
Communications	9	7.7%
Insurance	47	7.3
Manufacturing	153	7.2
Transportation	8	7.0
Utilities	52	6.6
Diversified service	17	6.5
Commercial banking	46	6.3
Trade	19	5.6
Energy and natural resources	15	3.7

Table 3: Salary Increase Budgets, 1988 and 1989

	1988		*Estimated for 1989*	
Type of Business	*Number of Companies**	*Median*	*Number of Companies*	*Median*
ALL INDUSTRIES				
Nonexempt	615	4.8%	372	4.8%
Exempt	631	5.0	377	5.0
Executive	584	5.4	357	5.3
MANUFACTURING				
Nonexempt	245	4.6	157	4.7
Exempt	251	4.8	160	4.8
Executive	237	5.2	153	5.1
UTILITIES				
Nonexempt	87	4.2	47	4.2
Exempt	95	4.5	50	4.7
Executive	74	5.2	43	5.2
INSURANCE				
Nonexempt	87	5.7	48	5.6
Exempt	87	5.8	48	5.7
Executive	83	6.3	45	6.1
COMMERCIAL BANKING				
Nonexempt	94	5.0	53	4.9
Exempt	94	5.0	52	5.0
Executive	90	5.3	51	5.3
TRADE				
Nonexempt	31	5.0	20	4.9
Exempt	31	5.0	20	4.9
Executive	31	5.3	19	5.0

* Other industry groups are included in totals but not shown separately because of small samples.

Chapter 2

Executive Incentive Compensation

This chapter examines the four major forms of executive incentive compensation, which are defined as follows:

Annual bonus: Generally, a percentage of profits is used to create a fund that is apportioned among the eligible executives based on individual contributions to profitability.

Restricted Stock: Shares of company stock are awarded to executives and are subject to restrictions as to sale or transfer, usually for three to five years. Additional restrictions often call for forfeiture if the executive terminates employment during the restricted period.

Long-term Performance Plans: Under these plans executives are awarded contingent grants of cash (long-term performance *units*) or stock (long-term performance *shares*). The payment of the award usually depends on the achievement of three-to-five-year financial performance goals.

Stock Options: These arrangements provide executives a right to purchase shares of company stock at a fixed price over a stated period of time. "Incentive stock options" (ISOs) meet Internal Revenue Code requirements, while "nonqualified stock options" do not. An option plan may allow "stock swaps" where previously acquired shares are used to exercise an option. "Stock appreciation rights" (SARs) may be attached to stock options. The SAR gives an optionee, in lieu of exercising the stock option, the right to receive an amount equal to the appreciation in the stock price since the date of grant.

To indicate trends in the incidence of these plans, the number reported in the 1988 survey is compared with the number reported in the 1983 survey. A five-year span is believed to be a good indicator of such trends. It should be noted that while the companies in the two surveys are not identical, the sample is relatively constant.

Table 4: Prevalence of Annual Bonus Plans

	May, 1988			*May, 1983*
		With Bonus Plan		*Percent With*
Industry Category	*Total Companies*	*Number*	*Percent*	*Bonus Plan*
Transportation	16	16	100%	*
Diversified service	24	23	96	*
Manufacturing	254	242	95	94%
Energy	31	29	94	*
Commercial banking	93	83	89	70
Insurance	91	81	89	62
Communications	17	15	88	*
Trade	33	29	88	72
Utilities	111	72	65	33

* Data not available

Table 5: Prevalence of Bonus Awards

		Percent that Paid Bonus	
Industry Category	*Total Plans*	*1987*	*1986*
Manufacturing	242	84%	86%
Insurance	81	83	86
Commercial banking	83	83	87
Diversified service	23	83	83
Transportation	16	81	81
Energy	29	79	69
Utilities	72	78	74
Trade	29	76	69
Communications	15	73	73

Table 6: Median CEO Bonus Awards for 1987

Industry Category	*Number of CEOS*	*Percentage of Salary*
Manufacturing	220	68%
Diversified service	21	60
Transportation	11	60
Energy	21	53
Communications	14	50
Trade	24	49
Insurance	66	47
Commercial banking	65	37
Utilities	58	31

Table 7: Prevalence of Restricted Stock Plans

	May, 1988			*May, 1983*
		With Restricted Stock		*Percent with*
Industry Category	*Total Companies*	*Number*	*Percent*	*Restricted Stock*
Diversified service	24	11	46	*
Energy	31	13	42	*
Commercial banking	93	30	32	12%
Manufacturing	254	77	30	27
Trade	33	10	30	25
Insurance: stock	68	14	21	23
Transportation	16	3	19	*
Communications	17	2	12	*
Utilities	111	12	11	5

* Data not available

Table 8: Median Restricted Stock Awards for 1987 to The Five Highest-Paid Executives as a Group

*Industry Category**	*Number of Companies*	*Number of Executives*	*Median*
Insurance: stock	7	23	54%
Manufacturing	37	149	52
Commercial banking	15	55	46
Diversified service	5	16	44
Energy	8	26	37
Utilities	6	21	28

* Insufficient data for industries not shown.

Table 9: Prevalence of Long-Term Performance Plans

	May, 1988			*May, 1983*
		With Long-term Performance Plans		*Percent with Long-term*
Industry Category	*Total Companies*	*Number*	*Percent*	*Performance Plans*
Energy	31	12	39%	*
Diversified service	24	9	38	*
Manufacturing	254	90	35	33%
Communications	17	5	29	*
Commercial banking	93	22	24	15
Insurance	91	22	24	12
Utilities	111	27	24	5
Transportation	16	2	13	*
Trade	33	4	12	12

* Data not available

Table 10: Types of Long-Term Performance Plans

		Number and Percent of Plans by Type					
	Total Plans	*Both Unit and Share Plans*		*Only Unit Plan*		*Only Share Plan*	
Industry Category	*Number*	*Number*	*Percent*	*Number*	*Percent*	*Number*	*Percent*
Manufacturing	90	6	7%	58	64%	26	29%
Utilities	27	1	4	12	44	14	52
Commercial banking	22	4	18	11	50	7	32
Insurance	22	3	14	12	55	7	32
Energy	12	1	8	6	50	5	42
Diversified service	9	1	11	3	33	5	56
Communications	5	—	—	4	80	1	20
Trade	4	—	—	4	100	—	—
Transportation	2	—	—	2	100	—	—

Table 11: Median Long-Term Performance Awards for 1987 To The Five Highest-Paid Executives as a Group

*Industry Category**	*Number of Companies*	*Number of Executives*	*Median*
Energy	8	40	60%
Manufacturing	62	286	60
Diversified service	4	18	59
Commercial banking	14	63	45
Insurance	10	46	40
Utilities	17	73	32

* Insufficient data for industries not shown.

Table 12: Median Long-Term Performance Payments for 1987 To the Five Highest-Paid Executives as a Group

*Industry Category**	*Number of Companies*	*Number of Executives*	*Median*
Commercial banking	10	43	44%
Manufacturing	41	179	43
Diversified service	6	21	37
Energy	5	25	29
Insurance	9	44	26
Utilities	15	64	19

* Insufficient data for industries not shown.

Table 13: Prevalence of Stock Option Plans

	May, 1988			*May, 1983*
		With Stock Option Plan		*Percent with Stock Option Plan*
Industry Category	*Total Companies*	*Number*	*Percent*	
Communications	17	16	94%	*
Energy	31	26	84	*
Manufacturing	254	211	83	80%
Diversified service	24	19	79	*
Trade	33	26	79	63
Commercial banking	93	65	70	44
Transportation	16	11	69	*
Insurance: stock	68	34	50	48
Utilities	111	39	35	20

*Data not available.

Table 14: Types of Options

		Number and Percent of Plans by Type					
	Total Plans	*Both ISO and Nonqualified*		*Only ISO*		*Only Nonqualified*	
Industry Category	*Number*	*Number*	*Percent*	*Number*	*Percent*	*Number*	*Percent*
Manufacturing	211	146	69%	16	8%	47	22%
Commercial banking	65	52	80	4	6	7	11
Utilities	39	28	72	3	8	7	18
Insurance: stock	34	24	71	2	6	7	21
Energy	26	17	65	3	12	6	23
Trade	26	16	62	4	15	6	23
Diversified service	19	12	63	—	—	7	37
Communications	16	11	69	3	19	1	6
Transportation	11	9	82	—	—	2	18

Table 15: 1987 Stock Option Grants

Industry Category	*Companies with Stock Option Plan*	*Granted Options in 1987*	
		Number	*Percent*
Energy	26	21	81%
Commercial banking	65	52	80
Insurance: stock	34	27	79
Manufacturing	211	165	78
Trade	26	19	73
Utilities	39	26	67
Transportation	11	7	64
Communications	16	10	63
Diversified service	19	12	63

Table 16: 1987 Stock Option Grants by Type

		Type of Option Granted					
	Total Responses	*Both ISO and Nonqualifed*		*ISO Only*		*Nonqualified Only*	
Industry Category	*Number*	*Number*	*Percent*	*Number*	*Percent*	*Number*	*Percent*
Manufacturing	159	52	33%	13	8%	94	59%
Commercial banking	51	25	49	7	14	19	37
Insurance: stock	26	8	31	3	12	15	58
Utilities	25	7	28	3	12	15	60
Energy	19	6	32	2	11	11	58
Trade	18	2	11	7	39	9	50
Diversified service	11	1	9	—	—	10	91
Communications	9	1	11	2	22	6	67
Transportation	7	1	14	1	14	5	71

Table 17: Incentive Stock Options with Stock Swap— Stock Appreciation Rights

Industry Category	ISO Plans Number	With Stock Swap Number	With Stock Swap Percent	With SAR Number	With SAR Percent
Manufacturing	162	110	68%	81	50%
Commercial banking	56	33	59	26	46
Utilities	31	15	48	14	45
Insurance: stock	26	16	62	16	62
Energy	20	14	70	12	60
Trade	20	13	65	7	35
Communications	14	7	50	5	36
Diversified service	12	6	50	5	42
Transportation	9	6	67	5	56

Table 18: Nonqualified Options with Stock Swap— Stock Appreciation Rights

Industry Category	Nonqualified Options Number	With Stock Swap Number	With Stock Swap Percent	With SAR Number	With SAR Percent
Manufacturing	193	118	61%	94	49%
Commercial banking	59	34	58	27	46
Utilities	35	15	43	17	49
Insurance: stock	31	16	52	16	52
Energy	23	16	70	14	61
Trade	22	15	68	9	41
Diversified service	19	10	53	7	37
Communications	12	6	50	4	33
Transportation	11	6	55	7	64

Table 19: Size of 1987 Stock Option Grants To The Five Highest-Paid Executives as a Group

			Size of Grant (Percent of Salary)		
				Middle 50% Range	
Industry Category	Number of Companies	Number of Executives	Median	Low	High
Transportation	5	22	250%	57%	470%
Energy	18	76	200	78	300
Manufacturing	149	681	141	78	235
Diversified service	11	46	132	78	232
Trade	16	67	123	66	202
Commercial banking	50	220	115	81	162
Utilities	22	96	107	73	152
Communications	8	39	102	85	129
Insurance: stock	23	103	89	45	152

Table 20: Gains at Exercise in 1987 of the Five Highest-Paid Executives as a Group

			Dollars			Percent of Salary		
				Middle 50% Range			Middle 50% Range	
Industry Category	Number of Companies	Number of Executives	Median	Low	High	Median	Low	High
Diversified service	10	31	$515,000	$150,000	$1,000,000	143%	48%	244%
Transportation	5	22	478,000	199,000	1,000,000	183	107	523
Communications	6	19	399,000	64,000	2,000,000	102	21	456
Energy	13	46	282,000	146,000	875,000	88	57	178
Manufacturing	103	353	256,000	92,000	644,000	82	38	199
Commercial banking	26	67	187,000	56,000	618,000	78	22	182
Insurance: stock	12	33	159,000	75,000	499,000	54	27	128
Trade	6	17	146,000	22,000	779,000	84	14	278
Utilities	20	49	82,000	47,000	187,000	36	17	68

Chapter 3

Compensation by Industry Category

The balance of the report contains the information listed below for each of the nine major industry categories and for eight manufacturing subcategories.

- Distribution of companies according to size;
- Median and low and high of middle 50 percent range for total current compensation and salary;
- Regression formulas for total current compensation and salary;
- Chart showing regression lines measuring the relationship between total current compensation and company size; and
- Total current compensation and salary of the second through fifth highest-paid executive as a percentage of CEO's (highest paid) pay.

With the exception of transportation and communications, where data were insufficient for analysis, each major industry section also contains an analysis relating bonus awards to company size and a table showing the size of bonus awards for each of the five executives. Life insurance and property and casualty insurance are analyzed in separate sections.

Executive Pay and Company Size

The regression line charts and the regression formulas are based on the generally accepted belief that there is a cause-and-effect relationship between company size and executive pay. The CEO of a large company is paid more than the CEO of a small company because the large company CEO has a more difficult and demanding job.

The regression lines on the charts measure the general relationship between total current compensation and company size. The lines can be used for determining the average compensation of executives for any company size. For greater precision, the regression formulas can be used. (See the Appendix for an explanation of how to use the formulas.)

Chapter 4
Manufacturing

Chart 1: Total Current Compensation of the Five Highest-Paid Executives, by Company Sales

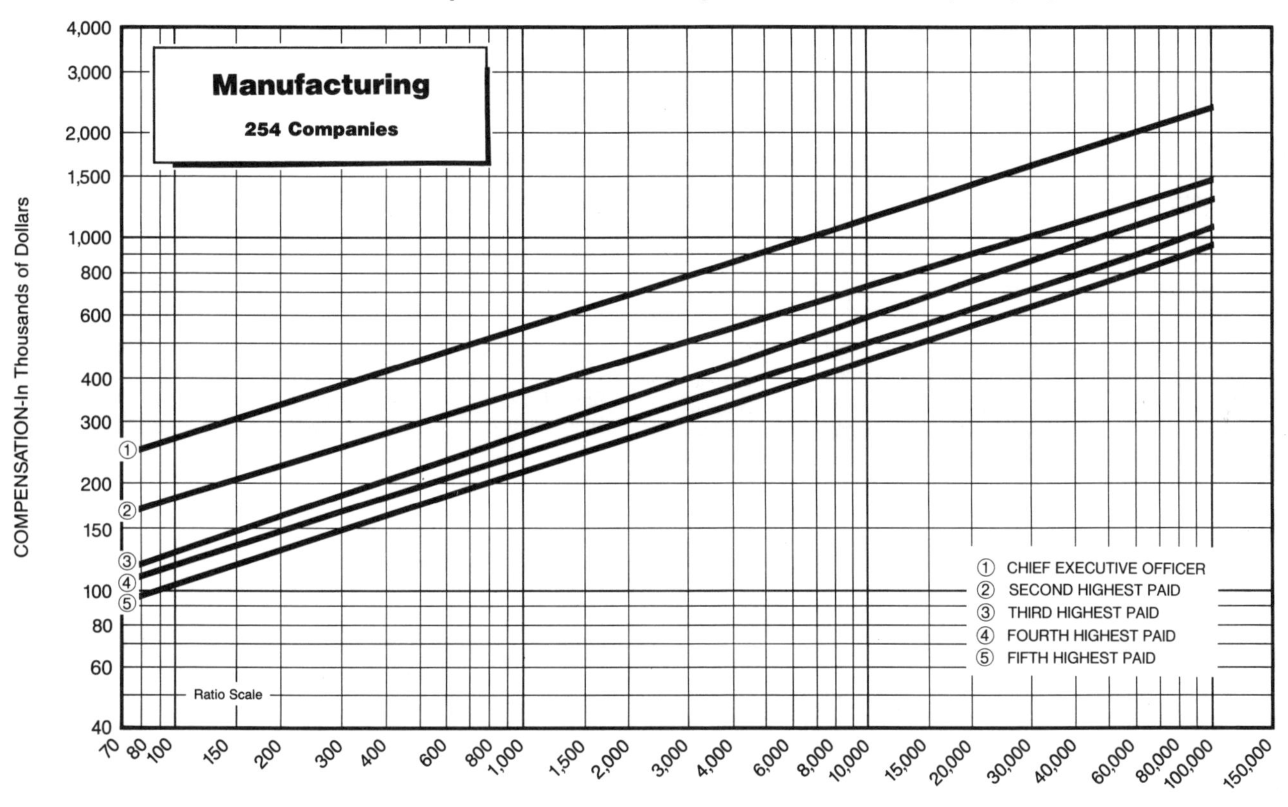

Table 21: 1987 Sales Volume

1987 Sales	Companies Number	Companies Percent
$5 billion and over	47	19%
2-4,999 billion	54	21
1-1,999 billion	50	20
500-999 million	36	14
300-499 million	30	12
200-299 million	17	7
199 million and under	20	8
TOTAL	254	100%

Median	Middle 50% Range Low	Middle 50% Range High
$1.4 billion	$481 million	$4.1 billion

Table 22: 1987 Total Current Compensation

Compensation Rank	Median	Middle 50% Range Low	Middle 50% Range High
CEO	$642,000	$380,000	$941,000
Second highest	400,000	276,000	639,000
Third highest	320,000	214,000	470,000
Fourth highest	283,000	180,000	400,000
Fifth highest	252,000	160,000	360,000

Table 23: 1987 Total Current Compensation Regression Formula

Compensation Rank	Formula	r^2
CEO	$\log Y = 1.8036 + 0.3123 \log X$	59%
Second highest	$\log Y = 1.6206 + 0.3127 \log X$	59
Third highest	$\log Y = 1.5158 + 0.3127 \log X$	65
Fourth highest	$\log Y = 1.4484 + 0.3166 \log X$	69
Fifth highest	$\log Y = 1.3923 + 0.3184 \log X$	69

Table 24: Total Current Compensation as a Percentage of CEO's Total Current Compensation*

		Middle 50% Range	
Compensation Rank	Median	Low	High
Second highest	66%	57%	76%
Third highest	52	44	60
Fourth highest	45	39	54
Fifth highest	40	34	48

* Please note that for all tables showing this relationship, the percentages are not based on the preceding table showing the median and the middle fifty percent range of total current compensation.

Table 25: 1987 Salary

		Middle 50% Range	
Compensation Rank	Median	Low	High
CEO	$410,000	$275,000	$540,000
Second highest	260,000	185,000	365,000
Third highest	213,000	154,000	289,000
Fourth highest	195,000	139,000	254,000
Fifth highest	175,000	130,000	238,000

Table 26: 1987 Salary Regression Formula

Compensation Rank	Formula	r^2
CEO	$\log Y = 1.7662 + 0.2621 \log X$	65%
Second highest	$\log Y = 1.5869 + 0.2646 \log X$	62
Third highest	$\log Y = 1.5015 + 0.2629 \log X$	68
Fourth highest	$\log Y = 1.4679 + 0.2580 \log X$	70
Fifth highest	$\log Y = 1.4309 + 0.2579 \log X$	71

Table 27: Salary as a Percentage of CEO's Salary*

		Middle 50% Range	
Compensation Rank	Median	Low	High
Second highest	67%	59%	78%
Third highest	54	48	62
Fourth highest	49	42	56
Fifth highest	45	38	52

* Please note that for all tables showing this relationship, the percentages are not based on the preceding table showing the median and middle fifty percent range of salary.

Table 28: 1987 Bonus Awards (as Percent of Salary), by Company Size

	Sales Volume		
	Middle 50% Range		
Executive	Low $481 Million	Median $1.4 Billion	High $4.1 Billion
CEO			
1987 Bonus	58%	66%	73%
Salary	$293,000	$387,000	$513,000
Second Highest			
1987 Bonus	51%	59%	67%
Salary	$198,000	$262,000	$348,000
Third Highest			
1987 Bonus	48%	54%	62%
Salary	$160,000	$213,000	$283,000
Fourth Highest			
1987 Bonus	42%	51%	61%
Salary	$144,000	$190,000	$251,000
Fifth Highest			
1987 Bonus	37%	47%	57%
Salary	$132,000	$174,000	$229,000

Table 29: 1987 Bonus Awards

1987 Bonus Awards (Percent of Salary)	*CEOS*		*Second Highest Paid*		*Third Highest Paid*		*Fourth Highest Paid*		*Fifth Highest Paid*	
	Number	*Percent*	*Number*	*Percent*	*Number*	*Percent*	*Number*	*Percent*	*Number*	*Percent*
100% or more	38	17%	23	10%	14	6%	14	6%	11	5%
90-99	12	6	12	5	12	5	6	3	4	2
80-89	23	11	18	8	17	8	17	8	9	4
70-79	33	15	34	15	24	11	21	9	16	7
60-69	35	16	27	12	26	12	26	12	31	14
50-59	16	7	40	18	32	14	30	13	28	13
40-49	14	6	19	8	35	16	40	18	39	18
30-39	21	10	17	8	26	12	31	14	25	11
20-29	12	6	16	7	20	9	18	8	29	13
10-19	12	6	18	8	14	6	17	8	26	12
Less than 10%	4	2	3	1	5	2	4	2	3	1
Total	220	100%	227	100%	225	100%	224	100%	221	100%
Median Bonus	68%		60%		53%		50%		48%	
Middle 50% Range	42 - 87%		41 - 78%		37 - 74%		34 - 70%		29 - 63%	

Chapter 5
Individual Manufacturing Industries

Aerospace

Chart 2: Total Current Compensation of the Five Highest-Paid Executives, by Company Sales

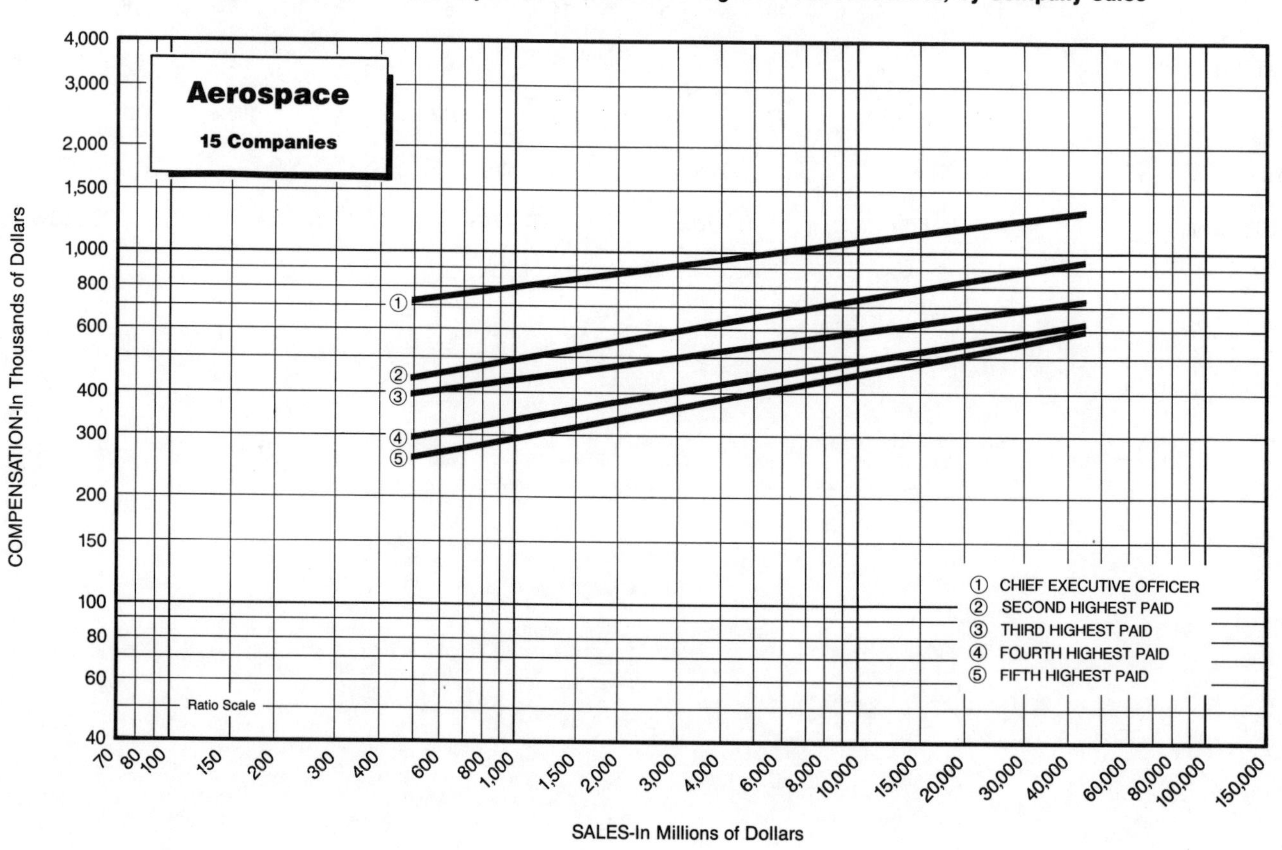

Table 30: 1987 Sales Volume

1987 Sales	Companies	
	Number	Percent
$5 billion and over	9	60%
2-4,999 billion	1	7
1-1,999 billion	4	27
500-999 million	—	—
300-499 million	1	7
Total	15	100%

Median	Middle 50% Range	
	Low	High
$6.8 billion	$1.6 billion	$13.1 billion

Table 31: 1987 Total Current Compensation

Compensation Rank	Median	Middle 50% Range	
		Low	High
CEO	$1,050,000	$808,000	$1,272,000
Second highest	660,000	534,000	792,000
Third highest	568,000	460,000	688,000
Fourth highest	443,000	385,000	539,000
Fifth highest	405,000	333,000	532,000

Table 32: 1987 Total Current Compensation Regression Formula

Compensation Rank	Formula	r^2
CEO	log Y = 2.4909 + 0.1364 log X	21%
Second highest	log Y = 2.1729 + 0.1726 log X	37
Third highest	log Y = 2.2387 + 0.1330 log X	21
Fourth highest	log Y = 2.0427 + 0.1622 log X	26
Fifth highest	log Y = 1.8952 + 0.1914 log X	28

Table 33: Total Current Compensation as a Percentage of CEO's Total Current Compensation

Compensation Rank	Median	Middle 50% Range	
		Low	High
Second highest	66%	59%	72%
Third highest	53	50	59
Fourth highest	42	38	50
Fifth highest	39	36	44

Table 34: 1987 Salary

Compensation Rank	Median	Middle 50% Range	
		Low	High
CEO	$523,000	$488,000	$650,000
Second highest	385,000	310,000	491,000
Third highest	323,000	277,000	400,000
Fourth highest	270,000	209,000	302,000
Fifth highest	250,000	232,000	302,000

Table 35: 1987 Salary Regression Formula

Compensation Rank	Formula	r^2
CEO	log Y = 2.4007 + 0.0918 log X	17%
Second highest	log Y = 2.1339 + 0.1181 log X	30
Third highest	log Y = 2.1991 + 0.0795 log X	16
Fourth highest	log Y = 2.0102 + 0.1121 log X	20
Fifth highest	log Y = 1.8808 + 0.1346 log X	34

Table 36: Salary as a Percentage of CEO's Salary

Compensation Rank	Median	Middle 50% Range	
		Low	High
Second highest	66%	62%	71%
Third highest	54	51	62
Fourth highest	44	39	54
Fifth highest	43	37	49

Consumer Chemicals

Chart 3: Total Current Compensation of the Five Highest-Paid Executives, by Company Sales

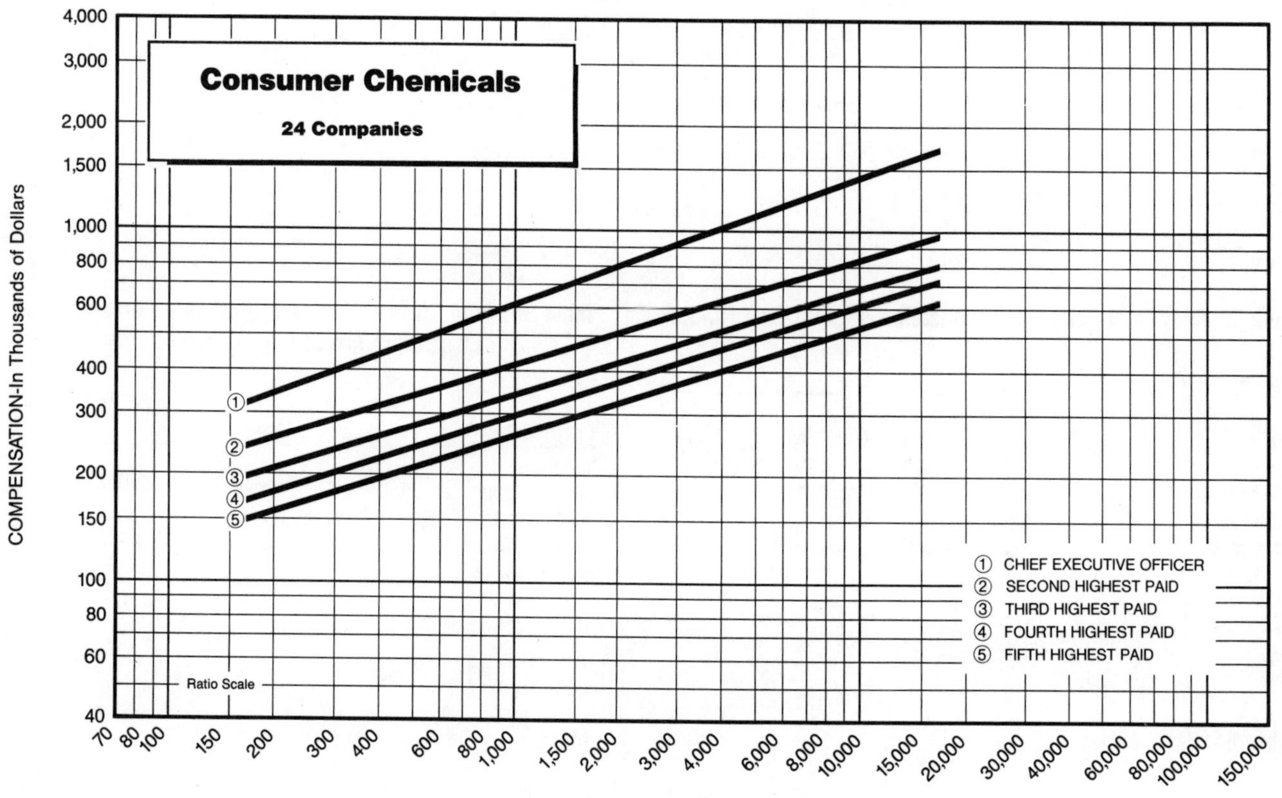

Table 37: 1987 Sales Volume

1987 Sales	*Companies* Number	*Companies* Percent
$5 billion and over	6	25%
2-4,999 billion	6	25
1-1,999 billion	5	21
500-999 million	4	17
300-499 million	2	8
200-299 million	—	—
199 million and under	1	4
Total	24	100%

Median	Middle 50% Range Low	Middle 50% Range High
$1.8 billion	$900 million	$4.9 billion

Table 38: 1987 Total Current Compensation

Compensation Rank	*Median*	*Middle 50% Range* Low	*Middle 50% Range* High
CEO	$1,009,000	$528,000	$1,200,000
Second highest	546,000	340,000	765,000
Third highest	495,000	285,000	585,000
Fourth highest	410,000	270,000	522,000
Fifth highest	375,000	263,000	459,000

Table 39: 1987 Total Current Compensation Regression Formula

Compensation Rank	Formula	r^2
CEO	$\log Y = 1.6847 + 0.3702 \log X$	64%
Second highest	$\log Y = 1.7148 + 0.3010 \log X$	54
Third highest	$\log Y = 1.6198 + 0.3043 \log X$	47
Fourth highest	$\log Y = 1.5161 + 0.3188 \log X$	64
Fifth highest	$\log Y = 1.5110 + 0.3043 \log X$	69

Table 40: Total Current Compensation as a Percentage of CEO's Total Current Compensation

		Middle 50% Range	
Compensation Rank	Median	Low	High
Second highest	61%	53%	79%
Third highest	51	47	58
Fourth highest	47	41	56
Fifth highest	41	34	48

Table 41: 1987 Salary

		Middle 50% Range	
Compensation Rank	Median	Low	High
CEO	$552,000	$374,000	$643,000
Second highest	317,000	230,000	404,000
Third highest	293,000	200,000	350,000
Fourth highest	271,000	185,000	314,000
Fifth highest	230,000	175,000	307,000

Table 42: 1987 Salary Regression Formula

Compensation Rank	Formula	r^2
CEO	$\log Y = 1.7896 + 0.2733 \log X$	63%
Second highest	$\log Y = 1.8022 + 0.2152 \log X$	46
Third highest	$\log Y = 1.7072 + 0.2218 \log X$	41
Fourth highest	$\log Y = 1.6173 + 0.2355 \log X$	59
Fifth highest	$\log Y = 1.5774 + 0.2327 \log X$	69

Table 43: Salary as a Percentage of CEO's Salary

		Middle 50% Range	
Compensation Rank	Median	Low	High
Second highest	65%	55%	80%
Third highest	54	49	63
Fourth highest	51	43	57
Fifth highest	43	39	52

Electrical Machinery

Chart 4: Total Current Compensation of the Five Highest-Paid Executives, by Company Sales

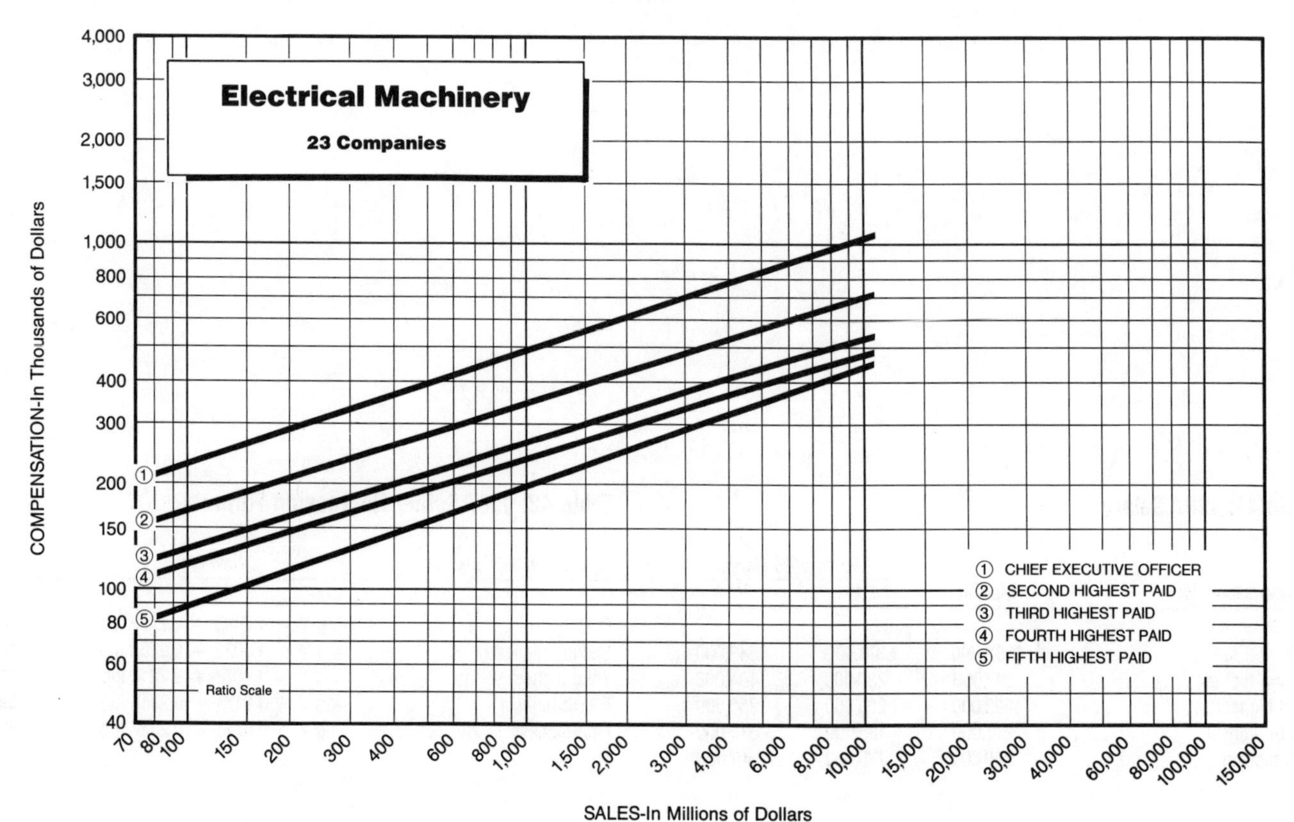

Table 44: 1987 Sales Volume

1987 Sales	*Companies* Number	Percent
$5 billion and over	4	17%
2-4,999 billion	3	13
1-1,999 billion	5	22
500-999 million	1	4
300-499 million	3	13
200-299 million	2	9
199 million and under	5	22
Total	23	100%

Median	Middle 50% Range Low	High
$1.2 billion	$223 million	$4.2 billion

Table 45: 1987 Total Current Compensation

Compensation Rank	*Median*	*Middle 50% Range* *Low*	*High*
CEO	$471,000	$281,000	$750,000
Second highest	350,000	175,000	569,000
Third highest	245,000	165,000	424,000
Fourth highest	209,000	152,000	363,000
Fifth highest	195,000	136,000	333,000

Table 46: 1987 Total Current Compensation Regression Formula

Compensation Rank	Formula	r^2
CEO	log Y = 1.7165 + 0.3264 log X	56%
Second highest	log Y = 1.6073 + 0.3108 log X	58
Third highest	log Y = 1.4832 + 0.3147 log X	74
Fourth highest	log Y = 1.4705 + 0.3019 log X	75
Fifth highest	log Y = 1.4109 + 0.3088 log X	69

Table 47: Total Current Compensation as a Percentage of CEO's Total Current Compensation

		Middle 50% Range	
Compensation Rank	Median	Low	High
Second highest	71%	61%	84%
Third highest	57	43	64
Fourth highest	50	40	59
Fifth highest	45	38	52

Table 48: 1987 Salary

		Middle 50% Range	
Compensation Rank	Median	Low	High
CEO	$287,000	$230,000	$500,000
Second highest	250,000	171,000	296,000
Third highest	180,000	133,000	240,000
Fourth highest	160,000	135,000	223,000
Fifth highest	151,000	116,000	220,000

Table 49: 1987 Salary Regression Formula

Compensation Rank	Formula	r^2
CEO	log Y = 1.7604 + 0.2559 log X	56%
Second highest	log Y = 1.5783 + 0.2653 log X	58
Third highest	log Y = 1.4814 + 0.2662 log X	65
Fourth highest	log Y = 1.5542 + 0.2249 log X	70
Fifth highest	log Y = 1.4637 + 0.2457 log X	65

Table 50: Salary as a Percentage of CEO's Salary

		Middle 50% Range	
Compensation Rank	Median	Low	High
Second highest	68%	61%	87%
Third highest	54	46	69
Fourth highest	48	42	58
Fifth highest	47	36	57

Food and Kindred Products

Chart 5: Total Current Compensation of the Five Highest-Paid Executives, by Company Sales

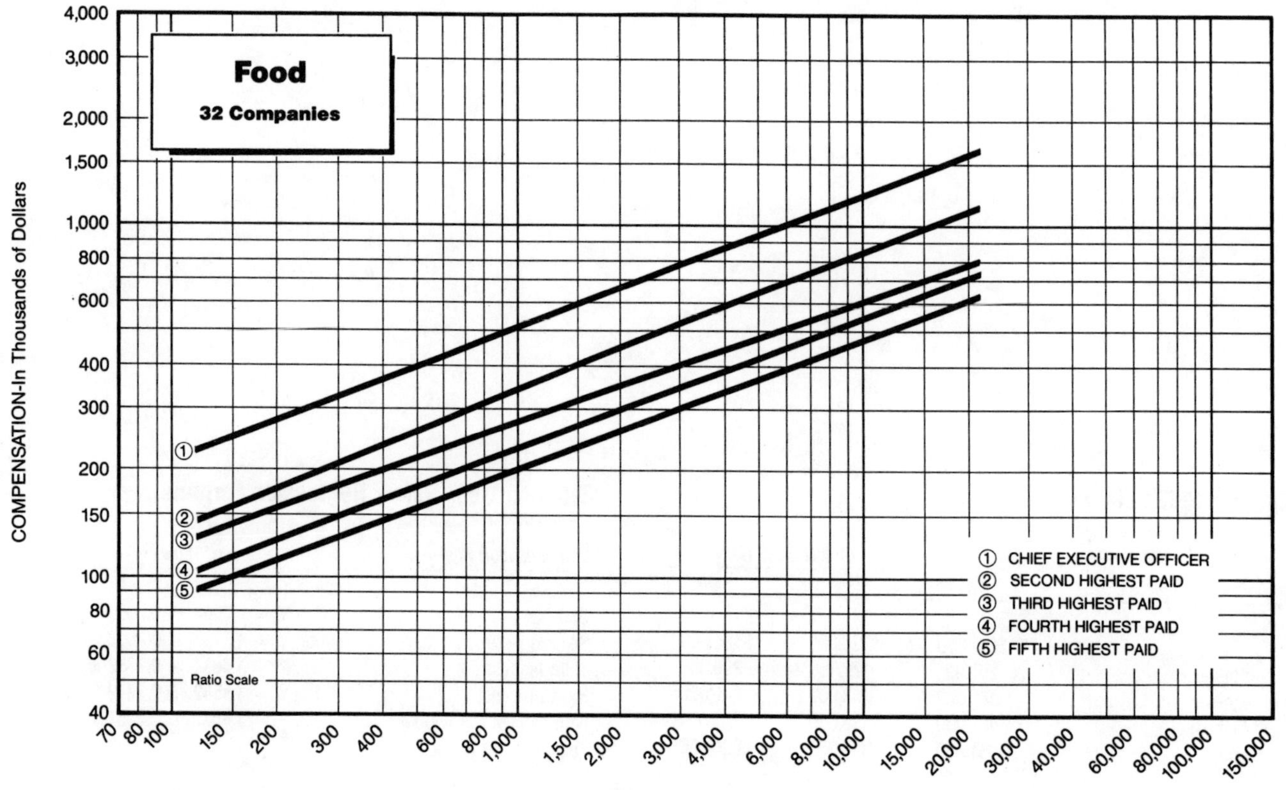

Table 51: 1987 Sales Volume

1987 Sales	Companies Number	Companies Percent
$5 billion and over	9	28%
2-4,999 billion	6	19
1-1,999 billion	8	25
500-999 million	5	16
300-499 million	3	9
200-299 million	—	—
199 million and under	1	3
Total	32	100%

Median	Middle 50% Range Low	Middle 50% Range High
$1.5 billion	$781 million	$5.9 billion

Table 52: 1987 Total Current Compensation

Compensation Rank	Median	Middle 50% Range Low	Middle 50% Range High
CEO	$725,000	$400,000	$1,131,000
Second highest	403,000	290,000	694,000
Third highest	328,000	221,000	574,000
Fourth highest	328,000	185,000	462,000
Fifth highest	266,000	181,000	420,000

Table 53: 1987 Total Current Compensation Regression Formula

Compensation Rank	Formula	r^2
CEO	log Y = 1.5831 + 0.3755 log X	62%
Second highest	log Y = 1.3698 + 0.3859 log X	61
Third highest	log Y = 1.3868 + 0.3506 log X	66
Fourth highest	log Y = 1.2715 + 0.3675 log X	70
Fifth highest	log Y = 1.3109 + 0.3403 log X	72

Table 54: Total Current Compensation as a Percentage of CEO's Total Current Compensation

Compensation Rank	Median	Middle 50% Range	
		Low	High
Second highest	67%	55%	76%
Third highest	50	42	63
Fourth highest	46	41	53
Fifth highest	41	34	49

Table 55: 1987 Salary

Compensation Rank	Median	Middle 50% Range	
		Low	High
CEO	$445,000	$285,000	$600,000
Second highest	300,000	205,000	380,000
Third highest	246,000	154,000	340,000
Fourth highest	228,000	152,000	275,000
Fifth highest	206,000	132,000	265,000

Table 56: 1987 Salary Regression Formula

Compensation Rank	Formula	r^2
CEO	log Y = 1.6151 + 0.3039 log X	68%
Second highest	log Y = 1.4111 + 0.3181 log X	59
Third highest	log Y = 1.4035 + 0.2947 log X	58
Fourth highest	log Y = 1.3507 + 0.2954 log X	66
Fifth highest	log Y = 1.3293 + 0.2902 log X	68

Table 57: Salary as a Percentage of CEO's Salary

Compensation Rank	Median	Middle 50% Range	
		Low	High
Second highest	70%	59%	78%
Third highest	57	46	63
Fourth highest	50	43	59
Fifth highest	46	39	52

Industrial Chemicals

Chart 6: Total Current Compensation of the Five Highest-Paid Executives, by Company Sales

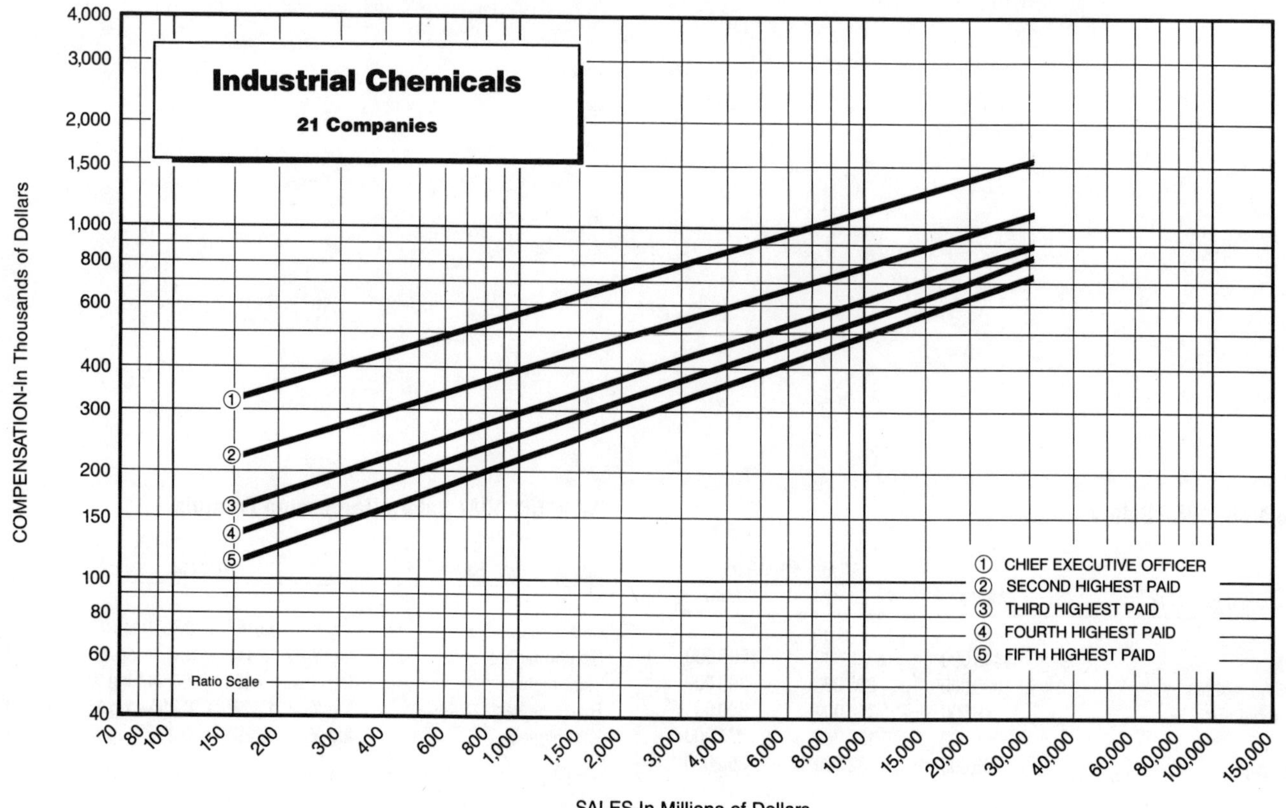

Table 58: 1987 Sales Volume

1987 Sales	*Companies* Number	Percent
$5 billion and over	4	19%
2-4,999 billion	6	29
1-1,999 billion	6	29
500-999 million	2	10
300-499 million	1	5
200-299 million	1	5
199 million and under	1	5
Total	21	100%

Median	Middle 50% Range Low	High
$1.7 billion	$1.2 billion	$2.6 billion

Table 59: 1987 Total Current Compensation

Compensation Rank	*Median*	*Middle 50% Range* *Low*	*High*
CEO	$726,000	$485,000	$954,000
Second highest	520,000	347,000	645,000
Third highest	406,000	230,000	508,000
Fourth highest	333,000	200,000	471,000
Fifth highest	255,000	170,000	393,000

Table 60: 1987 Total Current Compensation Regression Formula

Compensation Rank	*Formula*	r^2
CEO	log Y = 1.8952 + 0.2891 log X	69%
Second highest	log Y = 1.6998 + 0.2970 log X	58
Third highest	log Y = 1.4226 + 0.3440 log X	64
Fourth highest	log Y = 1.3496 + 0.3505 log X	74
Fifth highest	log Y = 1.3317 + 0.3399 log X	68

Table 61: Total Current Compensation as a Percentage of CEO's Total Current Compensation

		Middle 50% Range	
Compensation Rank	*Median*	*Low*	*High*
Second highest	67%	62%	74%
Third highest	53	48	60
Fourth highest	47	44	51
Fifth highest	40	34	46

Table 62: 1987 Salary

		Middle 50% Range	
Compensation Rank	*Median*	*Low*	*High*
CEO	$455,000	$365,000	$503,000
Second highest	289,000	225,000	395,000
Third highest	236,000	190,000	287,000
Fourth highest	200,000	151,000	266,000
Fifth highest	178,000	139,000	255,000

Table 63: 1987 Salary Regression Formula

Compensation Rank	*Formula*	r^2
CEO	log Y = 1.7177 + 0.2772 log X	67%
Second highest	log Y = 1.6230 + 0.2555 log X	61
Third highest	log Y = 1.4217 + 0.2851 log X	68
Fourth highest	log Y = 1.3675 + 0.2894 log X	79
Fifth highest	log Y = 1.3674 + 0.2784 log X	72

Table 64: Salary as a Percentage of CEO's Salary

		Middle 50% Range	
Compensation Rank	*Median*	*Low*	*High*
Second highest	69%	60%	74%
Third highest	55	52	60
Fourth highest	52	44	54
Fifth highest	47	41	52

Fabricated Metal Products

Chart 7: Total Current Compensation of the Five Highest-Paid Executives, by Company Sales

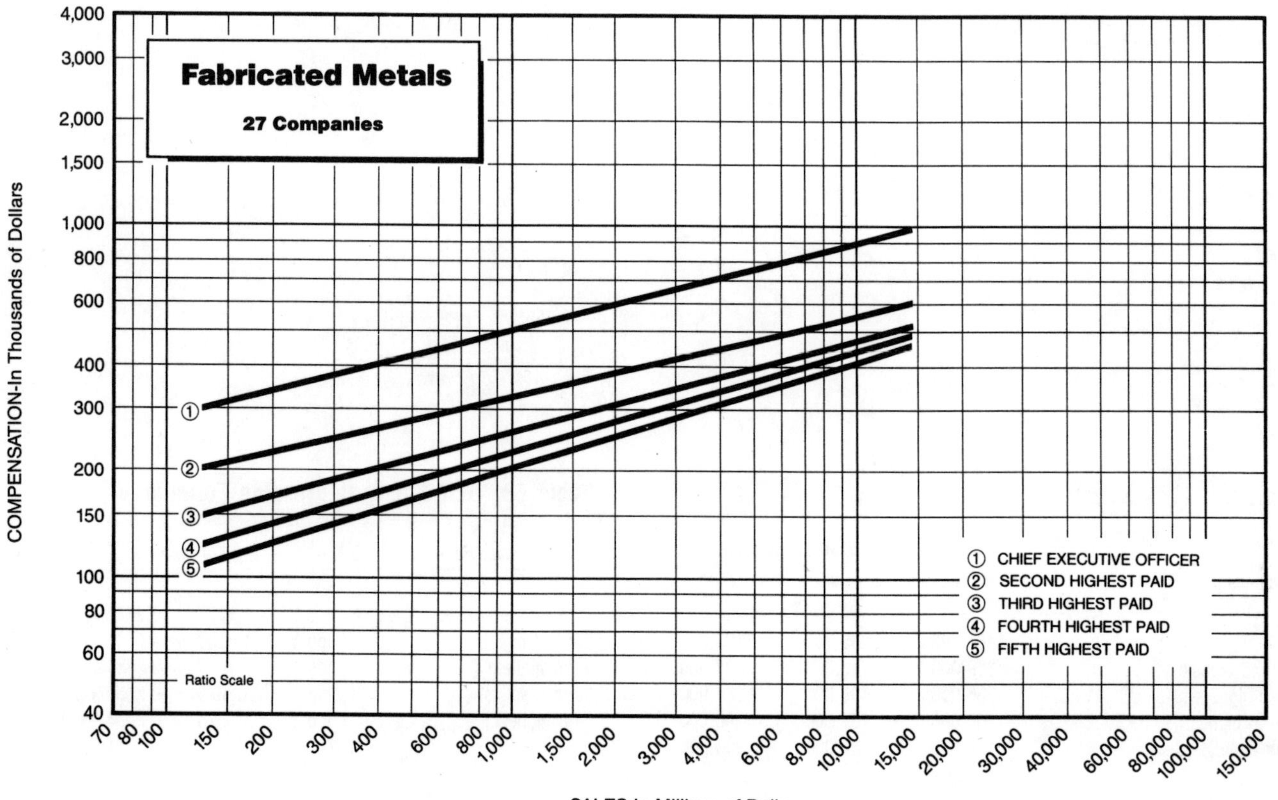

Table 65: 1987 Sales Volume

1987 Sales	*Companies* Number	Percent
$5 billion and over	1	4%
2-4,999 billion	4	15
1-1,999 billion	5	19
500-999 million	7	26
300-499 million	3	11
200-299 million	4	15
199 million and under	3	11
Total	27	100%

Median	Middle 50% Range Low	High
$693 million	$293 million	$1.8 billion

Table 66: 1987 Total Current Compensation

Compensation Rank	*Median*	*Middle 50% Range* *Low*	*High*
CEO	$485,000	$307,000	$644,000
Second highest	307,000	215,000	423,000
Third highest	249,000	178,000	304,000
Fourth highest	215,000	159,000	283,000
Fifth highest	196,000	147,000	252,000

Table 67: 1987 Total Current Compensation Regression Formula

Compensation Rank	*Formula*	r^2
CEO	log Y = 1.9550 + 0.2518 log X	45%
Second highest	log Y = 1.8296 + 0.2289 log X	32
Third highest	log Y = 1.6372 + 0.2600 log X	57
Fourth highest	log Y = 1.4903 + 0.2908 log X	66
Fifth highest	log Y = 1.4057 + 0.3023 log X	68

Table 68: Total Current Compensation as a Percentage of CEO's Total Current Compensation

		Middle 50% Range	
Compensation Rank	*Median*	*Low*	*High*
Second highest	65%	57%	78%
Third highest	50	39	61
Fourth highest	45	35	57
Fifth highest	40	30	51

Table 69: 1987 Salary

		Middle 50% Range	
Compensation Rank	*Median*	*Low*	*High*
CEO	$304,000	$250,000	$425,000
Second highest	204,000	172,000	246,000
Third highest	163,000	150,000	194,000
Fourth highest	146,000	111,000	174,000
Fifth highest	140,000	106,000	157,000

Table 70: 1987 Salary Regression Formula

Compensation Rank	*Formula*	r^2
CEO	log Y = 1.7013 + 0.2800 log X	70%
Second highest	log Y = 1.6255 + 0.2398 log X	49
Third highest	log Y = 1.4693 + 0.2616 log X	72
Fourth highest	log Y = 1.3657 + 0.2790 log X	78
Fifth highest	log Y = 1.3415 + 0.2755 log X	82

Table 71: Salary as a Percentage of CEO's Salary

		Middle 50% Range	
Compensation Rank	*Median*	*Low*	*High*
Second highest	64%	52%	76%
Third highest	51	42	59
Fourth highest	48	39	51
Fifth highest	43	38	51

Paper

Chart 8: Total Current Compensation of the Five Highest-Paid Executives, by Company Sales

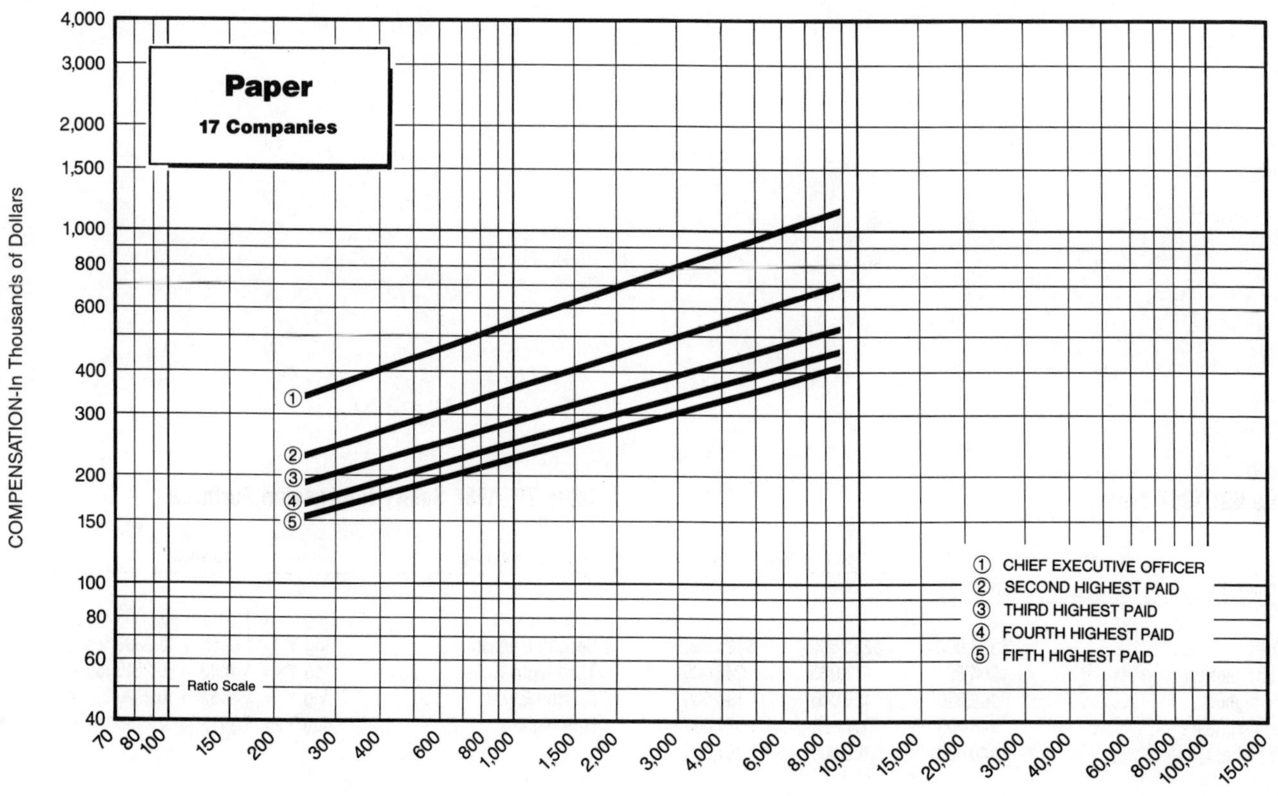

Table 72: 1987 Sales Volume

1987 Sales	Companies Number	Companies Percent
$5 billion and over	1	6%
2-4,999 billion	7	41
1-1,999 billion	3	18
500-999 million	3	18
300-499 million	1	6
200-299 million	2	12
Total	17	100%

Median	Middle 50% Range Low	Middle 50% Range High
$1.6 billion	$676 million	$4.2 billion

Table 73: 1987 Total Current Compensation

Compensation Rank	Median	Middle 50% Range Low	Middle 50% Range High
CEO	$663,000	$510,000	$925,000
Second highest	450,000	305,000	489,000
Third highest	365,000	238,000	447,000
Fourth highest	341,000	219,000	382,000
Fifth highest	318,000	200,000	343,000

Table 74: 1987 Total Current Compensation Regression Formula

Compensation Rank	Formula	r^2
CEO	log Y = 1.7313 + 0.3358 log X	65%
Second highest	log Y = 1.6009 + 0.3166 log X	62
Third highest	log Y = 1.6342 + 0.2751 log X	58
Fourth highest	log Y = 1.5955 + 0.2699 log X	57
Fifth highest	log Y = 1.5160 + 0.2819 log X	56

Table 75: Total Current Compensation as a Percentage of CEO's Total Current Compensation

		Middle 50% Range	
Compensation Rank	Median	Low	High
Second highest	70%	56%	75%
Third highest	51	44	59
Fourth highest	43	42	49
Fifth highest	41	37	45

Table 76: 1987 Salary

		Middle 50% Range	
Compensation Rank	Median	Low	High
CEO	$400,000	$338,000	$550,000
Second highest	285,000	205,000	338,000
Third highest	235,000	171,000	270,000
Fourth highest	209,000	155,000	220,000
Fifth highest	199,000	150,000	216,000

Table 77: 1987 Salary Regression Formula

Compensation Rank	Formula	r^2
CEO	log Y = 1.6558 + 0.2915 log X	61%
Second highest	log Y = 1.5202 + 0.2804 log X	54
Third highest	log Y = 1.5318 + 0.2484 log X	63
Fourth highest	log Y = 1.5774 + 0.2125 log X	54
Fifth highest	log Y = 1.5883 + 0.2068 log X	51

Table 78: Salary as a Percentage of CEO's Salary

		Middle 50% Range	
Compensation Rank	Median	Low	High
Second highest	66%	59%	79%
Third highest	53	49	65
Fourth highest	47	42	56
Fifth highest	47	40	53

Primary Metals

Chart 9: Total Current Compensation of the Five Highest-Paid Executives, by Company Sales

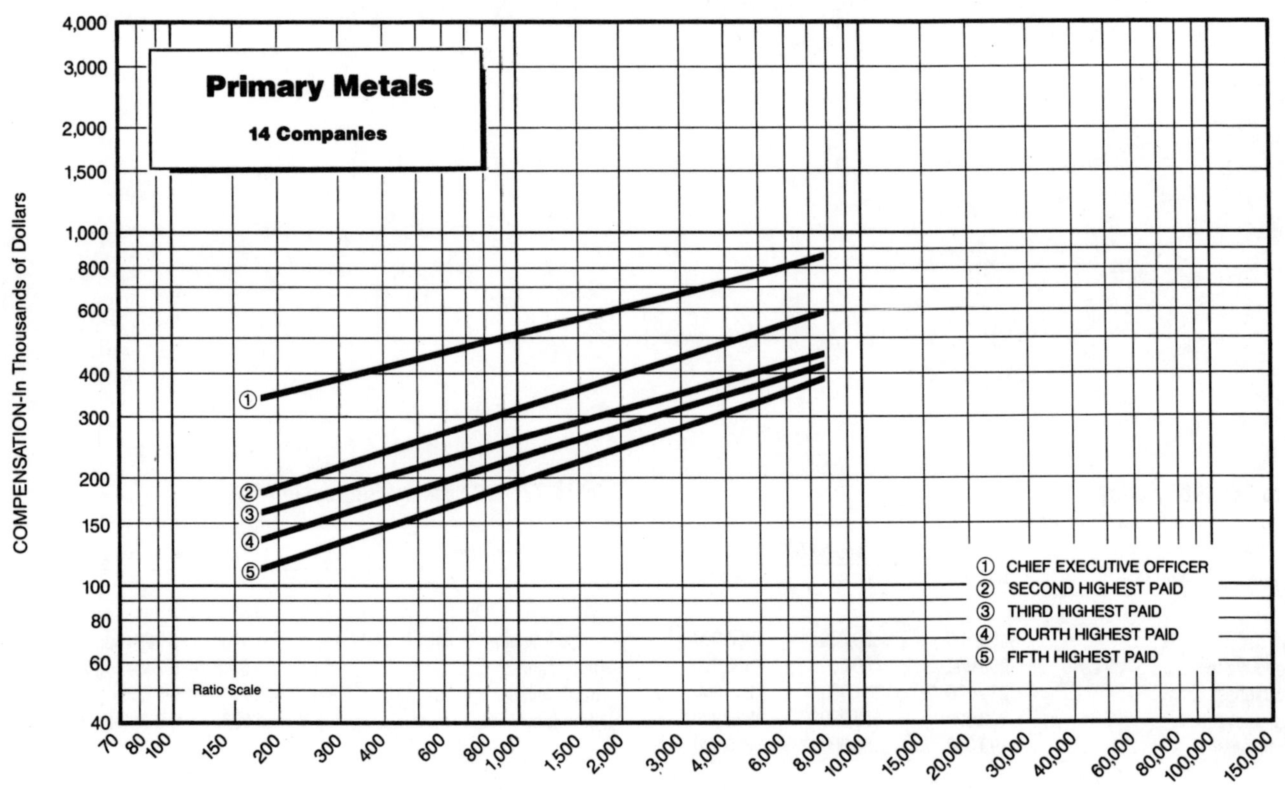

Table 79: 1987 Sales Volume

1987 Sales	*Companies* Number	Percent
$5 billion and over	2	14%
2-4,999 billion	3	21
1-1,999 billion	1	7
500-999 million	—	—
300-499 million	5	36
200-299 million	2	14
199 million and under	1	7
Total	14	100%

Median	Middle 50% Range Low	High
$463 million	$308 million	$4.3 billion

Table 80: 1987 Total Current Compensation

Compensation Rank	*Median*	*Middle 50% Range* *Low*	*High*
CEO	$559,000	$322,000	$671,000
Second highest	377,000	185,000	465,000
Third highest	261,000	170,000	366,000
Fourth highest	225,000	134,000	358,000
Fifth highest	181,000	120,000	333,000

Table 81: 1987 Total Current Compensation Regression Formula

Compensation Rank	*Formula*	r^2
CEO	log Y = 1.9651 + 0.2524 log X	52%
Second highest	log Y = 1.5970 + 0.3016 log X	60
Third highest	log Y = 1.6137 + 0.2675 log X	56
Fourth highest	log Y = 1.4613 + 0.3002 log X	63
Fifth highest	log Y = 1.3599 + 0.3158 log X	67

Table 82: Total Current Compensation as a Percentage of CEO's Total Current Compensation

		Middle 50% Range	
Compensation Rank	*Median*	*Low*	*High*
Second highest	60%	53%	73%
Third highest	51	46	56
Fourth highest	44	38	54
Fifth highest	40	33	49

Table 83: 1987 Salary

		Middle 50% Range	
Compensation Rank	*Median*	*Low*	*High*
CEO	$310,000	$230,000	$463,000
Second highest	189,000	141,000	301,000
Third highest	154,000	132,000	240,000
Fourth highest	152,000	107,000	220,000
Fifth highest	127,000	101,000	215,000

Table 84: 1987 Salary Regression Formula

Compensation Rank	*Formula*	r^2
CEO	log Y = 1.7806 + 0.2501 log X	79%
Second highest	log Y = 1.6530 + 0.2249 log X	61
Third highest	log Y = 1.5358 + 0.2369 log X	86
Fourth highest	log Y = 1.4349 + 0.2567 log X	82
Fifth highest	log Y = 1.3982 + 0.2595 log X	74

Table 85: Salary as a Percentage of CEO's Salary

		Middle 50% Range	
Compensation Rank	*Median*	*Low*	*High*
Second highest	61%	56%	73%
Third highest	56	45	59
Fourth highest	47	42	54
Fifth highest	45	38	49

Chapter 6

Commercial Banking

Chart 10: Total Current Compensation of the Five Highest-Paid Executives, by Total Assets

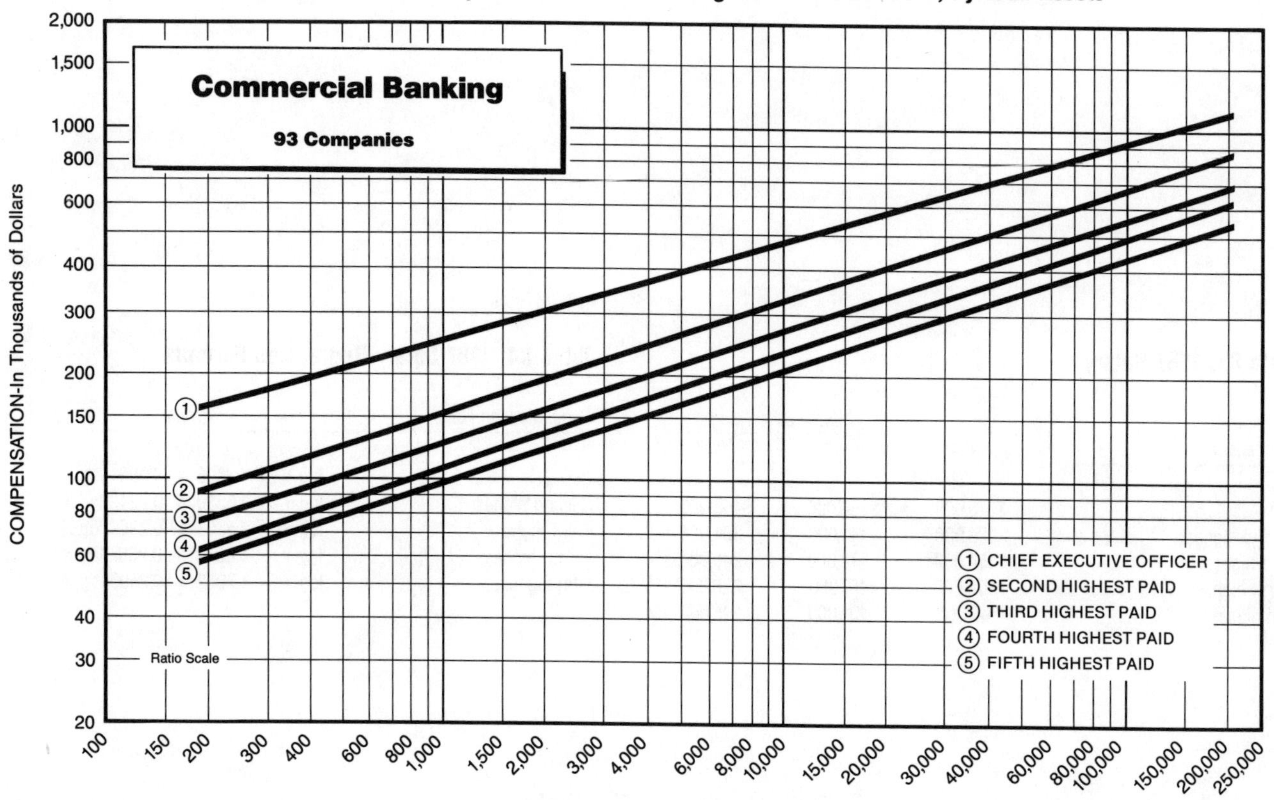

Table 86: 1987 Total Assets

1987 Total Assets	*Companies* Number	*Companies* Percent
$5 billion and over	49	53%
2-4,999 billion	18	19
1-1,999 billion	16	17
500-999 million	8	9
499 million and under	2	2
Total	93	100%

Median	Middle 50% Range Low	Middle 50% Range High
$5.2 billion	$1.6 billion	$11.7 billion

Table 87: 1987 Total Current Compensation

Compensation Rank	*Median*	*Middle 50% Range* Low	*Middle 50% Range* High
CEO	$412,000	$284,000	$575,000
Second highest	260,000	185,000	386,000
Third highest	215,000	149,000	326,000
Fourth highest	185,000	124,000	260,000
Fifth highest	166,000	107,000	230,000

Table 88: 1987 Total Current Compensation Regression Formula

Compensation Rank	Formula	r^2
CEO	log Y = 1.5692 + 0.2788 log X	50%
Second highest	log Y = 1.2353 + 0.3194 log X	57
Third highest	log Y = 1.1652 + 0.3170 log X	63
Fourth highest	log Y = 1.0461 + 0.3298 log X	62
Fifth highest	log Y = 1.0430 + 0.3171 log X	60

Table 89: Total Current Compensation as a Percentage of CEO's Total Current Compensation

		Middle 50% Range	
Compensation Rank	Median	Low	High
Second highest	67%	58%	75%
Third highest	57	47	63
Fourth highest	46	38	57
Fifth highest	42	35	49

Table 90: 1987 Salary

		Middle 50% Range	
Compensation Rank	Median	Low	High
CEO	$325,000	$235,000	$450,000
Second highest	215,000	158,000	295,000
Third highest	180,000	121,000	260,000
Fourth highest	153,000	115,000	230,000
Fifth highest	137,000	99,000	188,000

Table 91: 1987 Salary Regression Formula

Compensation Rank	Formula	r^2
CEO	log Y = 1.5449 + 0.2577 log X	56%
Second highest	log Y = 1.2877 + 0.2813 log X	58
Third highest	log Y = 1.1941 + 0.2850 log X	61
Fourth highest	log Y = 1.0776 + 0.3002 log X	65
Fifth highest	log Y = 1.0873 + 0.2851 log X	62

Table 92: Salary as a Percentage of CEO's Salary

		Middle 50% Range	
Compensation Rank	Median	Low	High
Second highest	69%	60%	75%
Third highest	58	49	65
Fourth highest	50	43	58
Fifth highest	44	37	52

Table 93: 1987 Bonus Awards (as Percent of Salary), by Company Size

	Total Assets		
	Middle 50% Range		
Executive	Low $1.6 Billion	Median $5.2 Billion	High $11.7 Billion
CEO			
1987 Bonus	35%	41%	46%
Salary	$246,000	$324,000	$391,000
Second Highest			
1987 Bonus	24%	34%	42%
Salary	$161,000	$216,000	$264,000
Third Highest			
1987 Bonus	25%	34%	40%
Salary	$131,000	$177,000	$218,000
Fourth Highest			
1987 Bonus	21%	29%	35%
Salary	$112,000	$153,000	$190,000
Fifth Highest			
1987 Bonus	20%	27%	33%
Salary	$103,000	$139,000	$171,000

Table 94: 1987 Bonus Awards

1987 Bonus Awards (Percent of Salary)	CEOS		Second Highest Paid		Third Highest Paid		Fourth Highest Paid		Fifth Highest Paid	
	Number	Percent	Number	Percent	Number	Percent	Number	Percent	Number	Percent
75 or more	8	12%	4	6%	4	6%	5	8%	4	6%
50-74	12	18	10	16	13	20	6	10	4	6
40-49	7	11	6	10	9	14	8	13	10	16
30-39	15	23	13	21	11	17	8	13	6	9
20-29	11	17	17	27	12	18	12	19	15	23
10-19	9	14	8	13	12	18	16	25	18	28
Less than 10%	3	5	5	8	5	8	8	13	7	11
Total	65	100%	63	100%	66	100%	63	100%	64	100%
Median Bonus	37%		31%		32%		25%		24%	
Middle 50% Range	25 - 51%		21 - 48%		18 - 50%		17 - 44%		13 - 43%	

Chapter 7
Communications

Chart 11: Total Current Compensation of the Five Highest-Paid Executives, by Company Sales

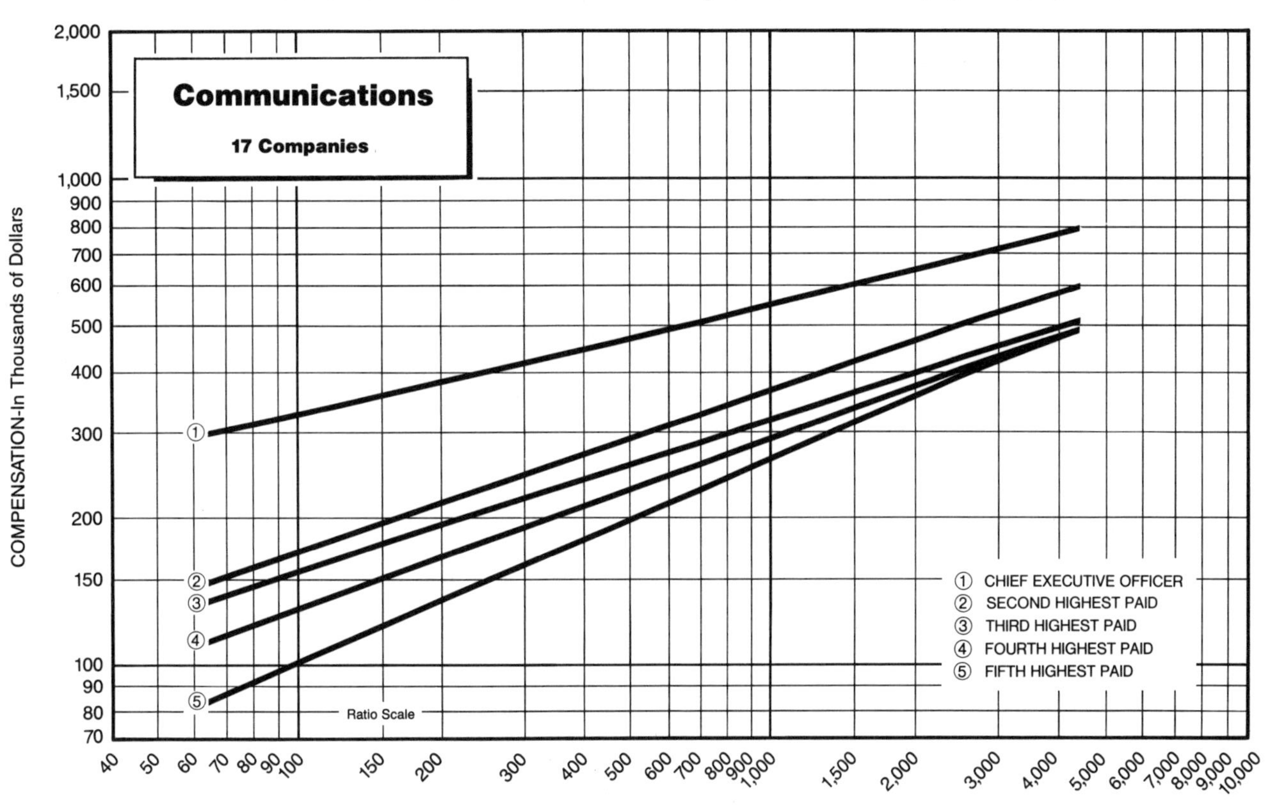

Table 95: 1987 Sales Volume

1987 Sales	*Companies* Number	*Companies* Percent
$2 billion and over	3	18%
1-1,999 billion	3	18
500-999 million	3	18
300-499 million	4	24
200-299 million	3	18
199 million and under	1	6
Total	17	100%

Median	Middle 50% Range Low	Middle 50% Range High
$551 million	$326 million	$1.7 billion

Table 96: 1987 Total Current Compensation

Compensation Rank	*Median*	*Middle 50% Range* Low	*Middle 50% Range* High
CEO	$420,000	$362,000	$721,000
Second highest	349,000	216,000	434,000
Third highest	293,000	198,000	381,000
Fourth highest	226,000	164,000	358,000
Fifth highest	190,000	154,000	309,000

Table 97: 1987 Total Current Compensation Regression Formula

Compensation Rank	*Formula*	r^2
CEO	log Y = 2.0685 + 0.2259 log X	28%
Second highest	log Y = 1.5837 + 0.3275 log X	40
Third highest	log Y = 1.5414 + 0.3213 log X	41
Fourth highest	log Y = 1.4143 + 0.3492 log X	52
Fifth highest	log Y = 1.1747 + 0.4142 log X	65

Table 98: Total Current Compensation as a Percentage of CEO's Total Current Compensation

		Middle 50% Range	
Compensation Rank	*Median*	*Low*	*High*
Second highest	67%	54%	76%
Third highest	54	46	66
Fourth highest	49	45	62
Fifth highest	46	41	51

Table 99: 1987 Salary

		Middle 50% Range	
Compensation Rank	*Median*	*Low*	*High*
CEO	$352,000	$320,000	$400,000
Second highest	234,000	180,000	289,000
Third highest	225,000	150,000	265,000
Fourth highest	198,000	150,000	227,000
Fifth highest	154,000	120,000	200,000

Table 100: 1987 Salary Regression Formula

Compensation Rank	*Formula*	r^2
CEO	log Y = 2.2276 + 0.1241 log X	22%
Second highest	log Y = 1.9076 + 0.1699 log X	32
Third highest	log Y = 1.5345 + 0.2749 log X	60
Fourth highest	log Y = 1.4747 + 0.2850 log X	68
Fifth highest	log Y = 1.2516 + 0.3437 log X	77

Table 101: Salary as a Percentage of CEO's Salary

		Middle 50% Range	
Compensation Rank	*Median*	*Low*	*High*
Second highest	67%	49%	75%
Third highest	55	42	64
Fourth highest	50	40	64
Fifth highest	47	40	57

Chapter 8

Diversified Service

Chart 12: Total Current Compensation of the Five Highest-Paid Executives, by Company Sales

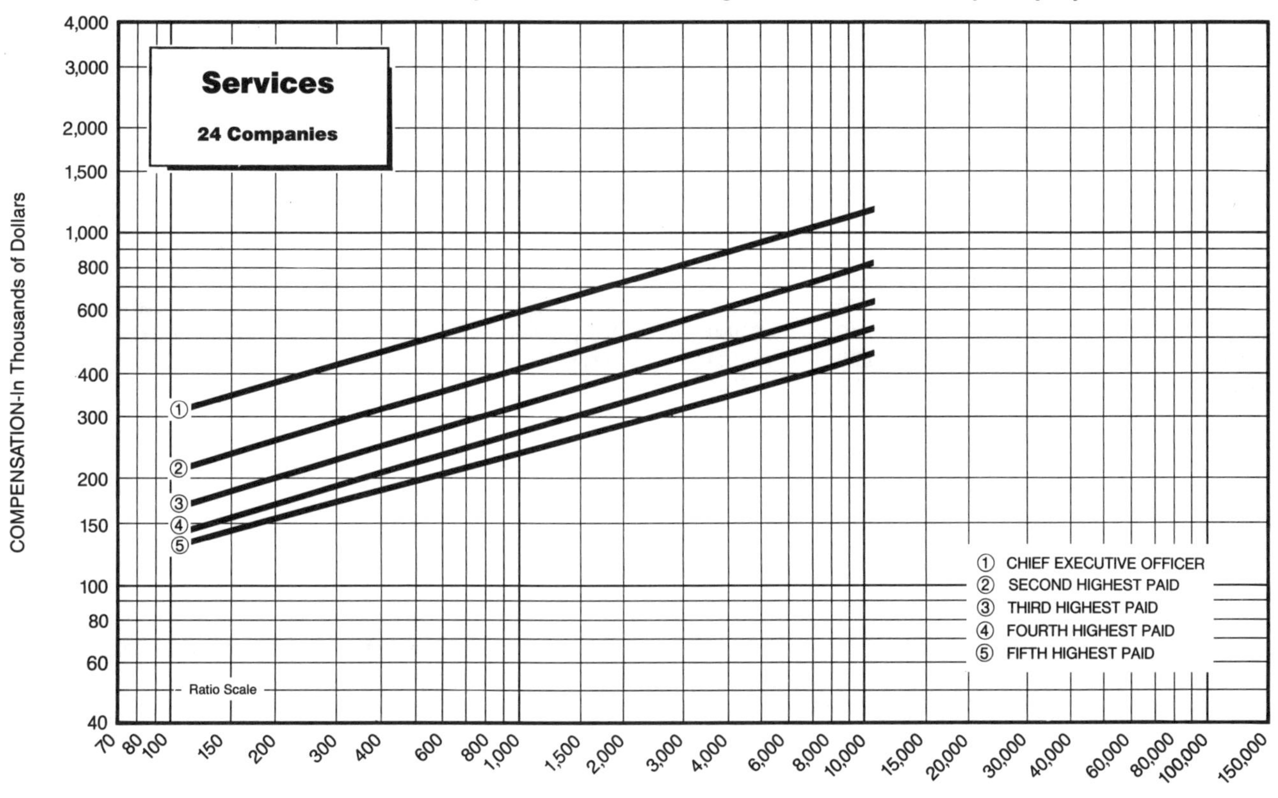

Table 102: 1987 Sales Volume

1987 Sales	*Companies* Number	*Companies* Percent
$5 billion and over	3	13%
2-4,999 billion	5	21
1-1,999 billion	1	4
500-999 million	9	38
300-499 million	1	4
200-299 million	1	4
199 million and under	4	17
Total	24	100%

Median	Middle 50% Range Low	Middle 50% Range High
$820 million	$344 million	$4.0 billion

Table 103: 1987 Total Current Compensation

Compensation Rank	*Median*	*Middle 50% Range* *Low*	*Middle 50% Range* *High*
CEO	$649,000	$418,000	$866,000
Second highest	451,000	317,000	592,000
Third highest	312,000	221,000	420,000
Fourth highest	275,000	196,000	400,000
Fifth highest	233,000	190,000	385,000

Table 104: 1987 Total Current Compensation Regression Formula

Compensation Rank	*Formula*	r^2
CEO	log Y = 1.9583 + 0.2737 log X	26%
Second highest	log Y = 1.7631 + 0.2862 log X	30
Third highest	log Y = 1.6680 + 0.2792 log X	31
Fourth highest	log Y = 1.5660 + 0.2903 log X	33
Fifth highest	log Y = 1.5433 + 0.2817 log X	31

Table 105: Total Current Compensation as a Percentage of CEO's Total Current Compensation

		Middle 50% Range	
Compensation Rank	*Median*	*Low*	*High*
Second highest	70%	61%	81%
Third highest	51	45	67
Fourth highest	44	41	60
Fifth highest	40	33	53

Table 106: 1987 Salary

		Middle 50% Range	
Compensation Rank	*Median*	*Low*	*High*
CEO	$421,000	$309,000	$575,000
Second highest	286,000	210,000	380,000
Third highest	227,000	165,000	300,000
Fourth highest	200,000	150,000	259,000
Fifth highest	157,000	150,000	247,000

Table 107: 1987 Salary Regression Formula

Compensation Rank	*Formula*	r^2
CEO	log Y = 1.9638 + 0.2117 log X	34%
Second highest	log Y = 1.8069 + 0.2183 log X	31
Third highest	log Y = 1.7477 + 0.1998 log X	27
Fourth highest	log Y = 1.6422 + 0.2199 log X	31
Fifth highest	log Y = 1.6140 + 0.2166 log X	27

Table 108: Salary as a Percentage of CEO's Salary

		Middle 50% Range	
Compensation Rank	*Median*	*Low*	*High*
Second highest	74%	69%	82%
Third highest	55	44	69
Fourth highest	48	44	63
Fifth highest	45	40	62

Table 109: 1987 Bonus Awards (as Percent of Salary), by Company Size

	Sales Volume		
		Middle 50% Range	
Executive	*Million*	*Million*	*Billion*
CEO			
1987 Bonus	51%	57%	69%
Salary	$356,000	$417,000	$560,000
Second Highest			
1987 Bonus	44%	52%	65%
Salary	$250,000	$297,000	$409,000
Third Highest			
1987 Bonus	42%	50%	66%
Salary	$193,000	$227,000	$305,000
Fourth Highest			
1987 Bonus	37%	42%	54%
Salary	$169,000	$204,000	$285,000
Fifth Highest			
1987 Bonus	29%	36%	48%
Salary	$156,000	$187,000	$261,000

Table 110: 1987 Bonus Awards

1987 Bonus Awards (Percent of Salary)	CEOS		Second Highest Paid		Third Highest Paid		Fourth Highest Paid		Fifth Highest Paid	
	Number	Percent	Number	Percent	Number	Percent	Number	Percent	Number	Percent
100% or more	2	10%	1	5%	2	11%	1	5%	1	6%
70-99	5	24	5	25	4	21	2	10	1	6
40-69	6	29	8	40	8	42	10	50	8	47
20-39	5	24	5	25	4	21	4	20	7	41
Less than 20%	3	14	1	5	1	5	3	15	—	—
Total	21	100%	20	100%	19	100%	20	100%	17	100%
Median Bonus	60%		59%		58%		50%		41%	
Middle 50% Range	33 - 75%		34 - 70%		34 - 75%		29 - 56%		30 - 55%	

Chapter 9

Energy and Natural Resources

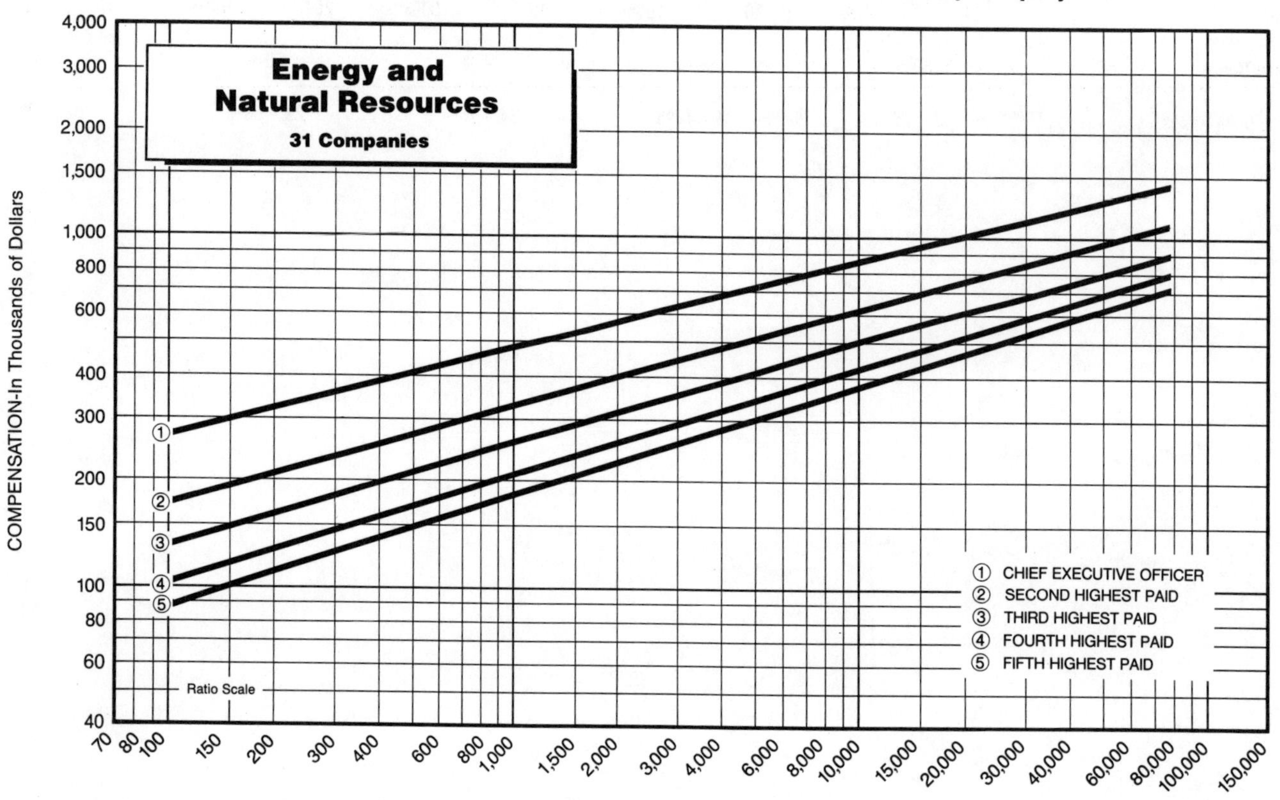

Table 111: 1987 Sales Volume

1987 Sales	*Companies* Number	Percent
$5 billion and over	11	35%
2-4,999 billion	1	3
1-1,999 billion	6	19
500-999 million	5	16
300-499 million	2	6
200-299 million	1	3
199 million and under	5	16
Total	31	100%

Median	Middle 50% Range Low	High
$1.4 billion	$417 million	$10.9 billion

Table 112: 1987 Total Current Compensation

Compensation Rank	*Median*	*Middle 50% Range* *Low*	*High*
CEO	$525,000	$318,000	$912,000
Second highest	400,000	206,000	665,000
Third highest	359,000	156,000	501,000
Fourth highest	213,000	144,000	409,000
Fifth highest	200,000	143,000	345,000

Table 113: Total Current Compensation Regression Formula

Compensation Rank	Formula	r^2
CEO	log Y = 1.9339 + 0.2483 log X	68%
Second highest	log Y = 1.6789 + 0.2768 log X	78
Third highest	log Y = 1.5857 + 0.2758 log X	70
Fourth highest	log Y = 1.4608 + 0.2911 log X	78
Fifth highest	log Y = 1.3355 + 0.3099 log X	81

Table 114: Total Current Compensation as a Percentage of CEO's Total Current Compensation

		Middle 50% Range	
Compensation Rank	Median	Low	High
Second highest	69%	64%	80%
Third highest	55	48	63
Fourth highest	49	40	53
Fifth highest	40	35	50

Table 115: 1987 Salary

		Middle 50% Range	
Compensation Rank	Median	Low	High
CEO	$525,000	$285,000	$625,000
Second highest	363,000	203,000	425,000
Third highest	244,000	144,000	379,000
Fourth highest	200,000	125,000	305,000
Fifth highest	190,000	109,000	275,000

Table 116: 1987 Salary Regression Formula

Compensation Rank	Formula	r^2
CEO	log Y = 2.0033 + 0.1892 log X	58%
Second highest	log Y = 1.7220 + 0.2284 log X	70
Third highest	log Y = 1.6047 + 0.2358 log X	66
Fourth highest	log Y = 1.5142 + 0.2416 log X	73
Fifth highest	log Y = 1.4192 + 0.2552 log X	76

Table 117: Salary as a Percentage of CEO's Salary

		Middle 50% Range	
Compensation Rank	Median	Low	High
Second highest	72%	64%	82%
Third highest	58	49	66
Fourth highest	50	42	59
Fifth highest	45	39	51

Table 118: 1987 Bonus Awards (as Percent of Salary), by Company Size

	Sales Volume		
	Middle 50% Range		
Executive	Low $417 Million	Median $1.4 Billion	High $10.9 Billion
CEO			
1987 Bonus	44%	48%	55%
Salary	$262,000	$351,000	$575,000
Second Highest			
1987 Bonus	34%	39%	48%
Salary	$180,000	$247,000	$421,000
Third Highest			
1987 Bonus	39%	42%	45%
Salary	$143,000	$200,000	$351,000
Fourth Highest			
1987 Bonus	30%	35%	45%
1987 Salary	$126,000	$176,000	$308,000
Fifth Highest			
1987 Bonus	31%	34%	42%
Salary	$108,000	$154,000	$277,000

Table 119: 1987 Bonus Awards

1987 Bonus Awards (Percent of Salary)	*CEOS*		*Second Highest Paid*		*Third Highest Paid*		*Fourth Highest Paid*		*Fifth Highest Paid*	
	Number	*Percent*	*Number*	*Percent*	*Number*	*Percent*	*Number*	*Percent*	*Number*	*Percent*
70-99	5	24%	2	9%	2	9%	2	9%	1	5%
40-69	9	43	9	41	9	41	9	41	9	45
20-39	6	29	9	41	10	46	11	50	7	35
Less than 20%	1	5	2	9	1	5	—	—	3	15
Total	21	100%	22	100%	22	100%	22	100%	20	100%
Median Bonus	53%		39%		38%		38%		39%	
Middle 50% Range	35 - 67%		31 - 59%		28 - 51%		29 - 57%		24 - 57%	

Chapter 10

Insurance

Chart 14: Total Current Compensation of the Five Highest-Paid Executives, by Premium Income

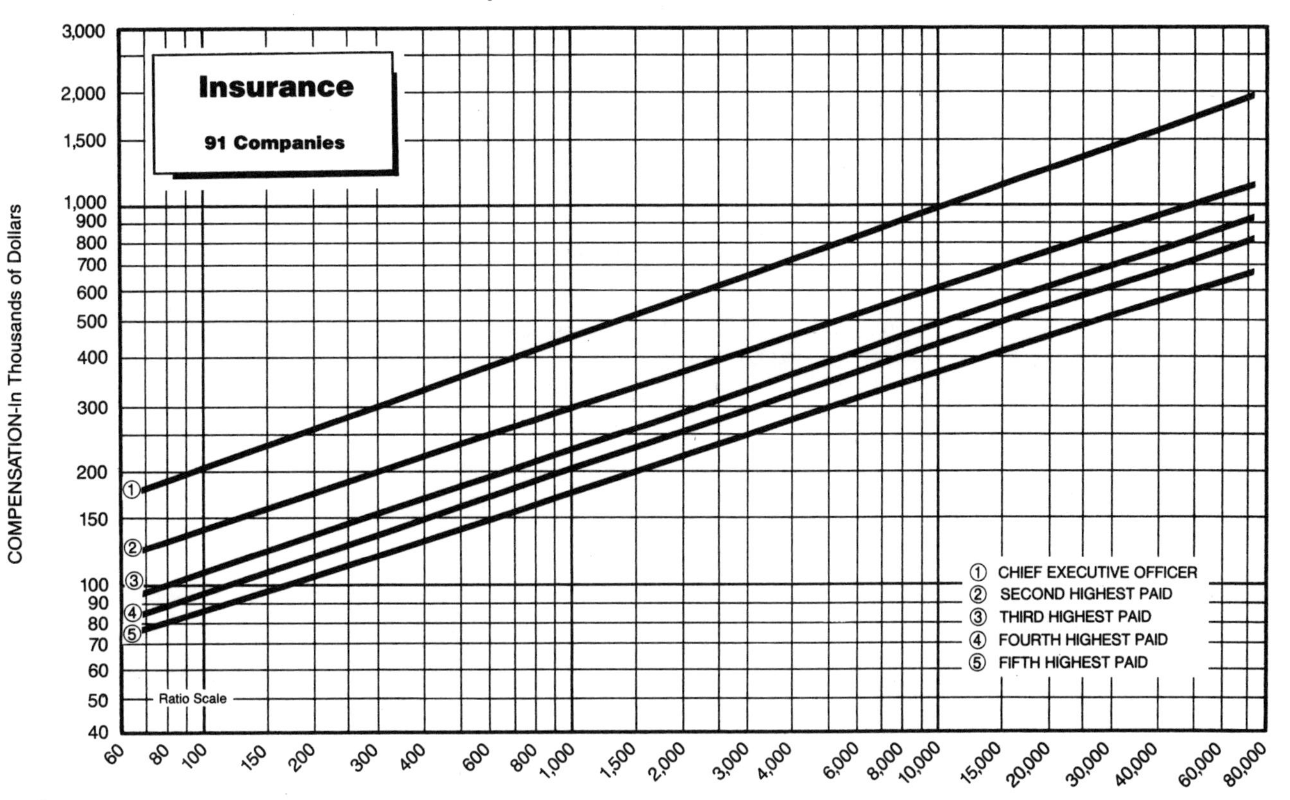

Table 120: 1987 Premium Income

1987 Premium Income	*Companies* Number	Percent
$5 billion and over	12	13%
2-4,999 billion	9	10
1-1,999 billion	17	19
500-999 million	12	13
300-499 million	14	15
200-299 million	8	9
199 million and under	19	21
Total	91	100%

Median	Middle 50% Range Low	High
$609 million	$213 million	$1.9 billion

Table 121: 1987 Total Current Compensation

Compensation Rank	*Median*	*Middle 50% Range* *Low*	*High*
CEO	$398,000	$258,000	$713,000
Second highest	255,000	176,000	390,000
Third highest	195,000	136,000	331,000
Fourth highest	167,000	126,000	298,000
Fifth highest	150,000	104,000	240,000

Table 122: 1987 Total Current Compensation Regression Formula

Compensation Rank	*Formula*	r^2
CEO	log Y = 1.6558 + 0.3341 log X	52%
Second highest	log Y = 1.5083 + 0.3202 log X	51
Third highest	log Y = 1.3937 + 0.3228 log X	58
Fourth highest	log Y = 1.3388 + 0.3241 log X	61
Fifth highest	log Y = 1.3044 + 0.3163 log X	63

Table 123: Total Current Compensation as a Percentage of CEO's Total Current Compensation

		Middle 50% Range	
Compensation Rank	*Median*	*Low*	*High*
Second highest	65%	56%	76%
Third highest	52	44	61
Fourth highest	46	39	56
Fifth highest	40	34	49

Table 124: 1987 Salary

		Middle 50% Range	
Compensation Rank	*Median*	*Low*	*High*
CEO	$284,000	$205,000	$448,000
Second highest	200,000	130,000	323,000
Third highest	153,000	105,000	250,000
Fourth highest	140,000	101,000	227,000
Fifth highest	129,000	88,000	189,000

Table 125: 1987 Salary Regression Formula

Compensation Rank	*Formula*	r^2
CEO	log Y = 1.6838 + 0.2797 log X	53%
Second highest	log Y = 1.5287 + 0.2714 log X	55
Third highest	log Y = 1.4088 + 0.2803 log X	62
Fourth highest	log Y = 1.3747 + 0.2775 log X	63
Fifth highest	log Y = 1.3561 + 0.2661 log X	63

Table 126: Salary as a Percentage of CEO's Salary

		Middle 50% Range	
Compensation Rank	*Median*	*Low*	*High*
Second highest	67%	57%	75%
Third highest	53	48	62
Fourth highest	50	42	55
Fifth highest	43	38	49

Table 127: 1987 Bonus Awards (as Percent of Salary), by Company Size

	Premium Income		
	Middle 50% Range		
Executive	*Low $213 Million*	*Median $609 Million*	*High $1.9 Billion*
CEO			
1987 Bonus	41%	49%	57%
Salary	$213,000	$284,000	$388,000
Second Highest			
1987 Bonus	36%	45%	52%
Salary	$143,000	$191,000	$263,000
Third Highest			
1987 Bonus	32%	38%	44%
Salary	$110,000	$152,000	$214,000
Fourth Highest			
1987 Bonus	28%	34%	42%
Salary	$101,000	$137,000	$191,000
Fifth Highest			
1987 Bonus	24%	31%	39%
Salary	$ 91,400	$122,000	$168,000

Table 128: 1987 Bonus Awards

1987 Bonus Awards (Percent of Salary)	CEOS		Second Highest Paid		Third Highest Paid		Fourth Highest Paid		Fifth Highest Paid	
	Number	Percent	Number	Percent	Number	Percent	Number	Percent	Number	Percent
100% or more	6	9%	7	10%	5	8%	3	5%	3	5%
70-99	11	17	8	12	3	5	4	6	3	5
50-69	11	17	11	16	12	18	13	20	9	15
40-49	9	14	9	13	8	12	7	11	6	10
30-39	8	12	11	16	12	18	14	22	12	20
20-29	8	12	6	9	11	16	5	8	12	20
10-19	9	14	9	13	11	16	12	19	10	16
Less than 10%	4	6	6	9	5	8	6	9	6	10
Total	66	100%	67	100%	67	100%	64	100%	61	100%
Median Bonus	47%		43%		34%		33%		32%	
Middle 50% Range	26 - 72%		24 - 68%		20 - 52%		16 - 50%		19 - 48%	

Life Insurance

Chart 15: Total Current Compensation of the Five Highest-Paid Executives, by Premium Income

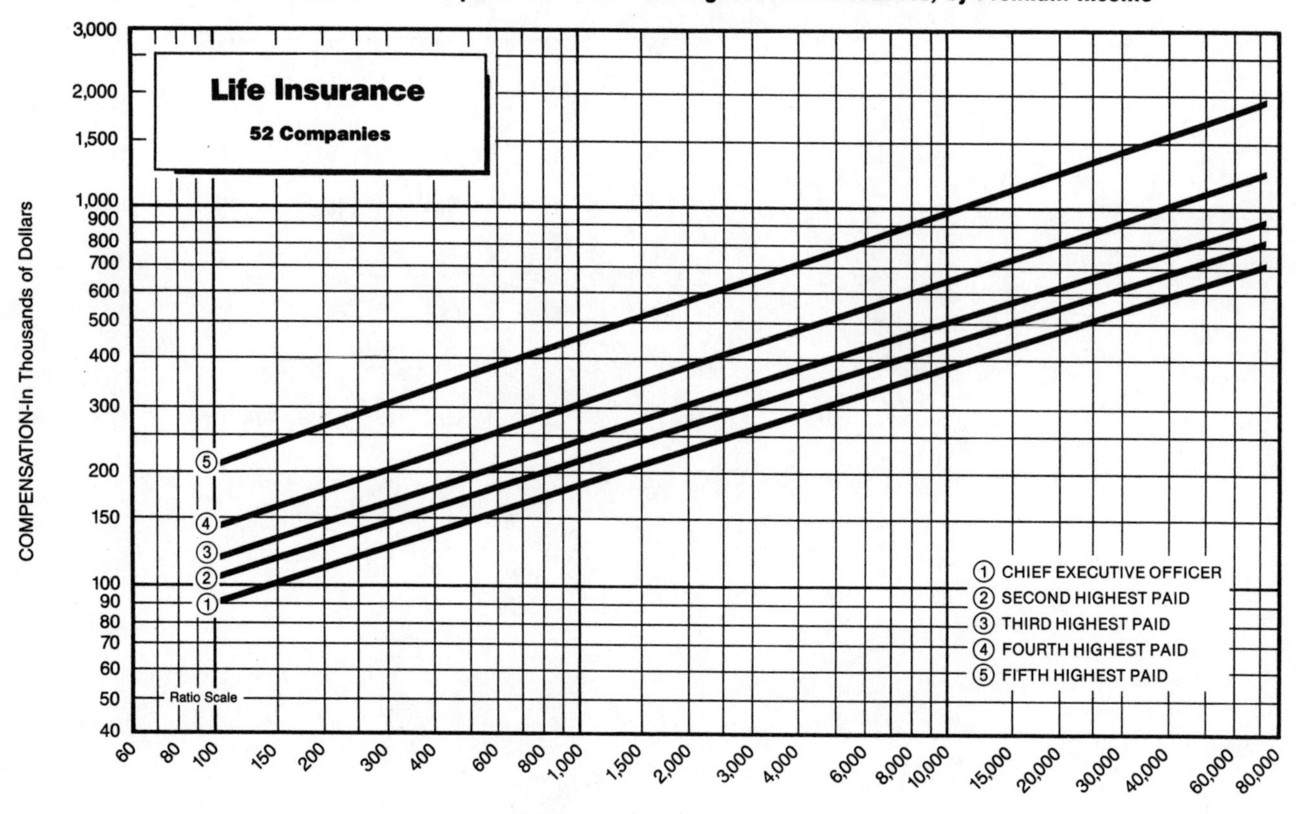

Table 129: 1987 Premium Income

1987 Premium Income	*Companies* Number	Percent
$5 billion and over	6	12%
2-4,999 billion	7	13
1-1,999 billion	13	25
500-999 million	6	12
300-499 million	6	12
200-299 million	5	10
199 million and under	9	17
Total	52	100%

Median	Middle 50% Range Low	High
$931 million	$248 million	$1.9 billion

Table 130: 1987 Total Current Compensation Regression Formula

Compensation Rank	*Formula*	r^2
CEO	$\log Y = 1.6363 + 0.3409 \log X$	52%
Second highest	$\log Y = 1.4894 + 0.3293 \log X$	55
Third highest	$\log Y = 1.4525 + 0.3110 \log X$	53
Fourth highest	$\log Y = 1.3699 + 0.3203 \log X$	58
Fifth highest	$\log Y = 1.3205 + 0.3164 \log X$	59

Table 131: 1987 Salary Regression Formula

Compensation Rank	*Formula*	r^2
CEO	$\log Y = 1.7120 + 0.2742 \log X$	51%
Second highest	$\log Y = 1.5517 + 0.2687 \log X$	61
Third highest	$\log Y = 1.4868 + 0.2622 \log X$	63
Fourth highest	$\log Y = 1.4255 + 0.2684 \log X$	67
Fifth highest	$\log Y = 1.3980 + 0.2586 \log X$	65

Property and Casualty Insurance

Chart 16: Total Current Compensation of the Five Highest-Paid Executives, by Premium Income

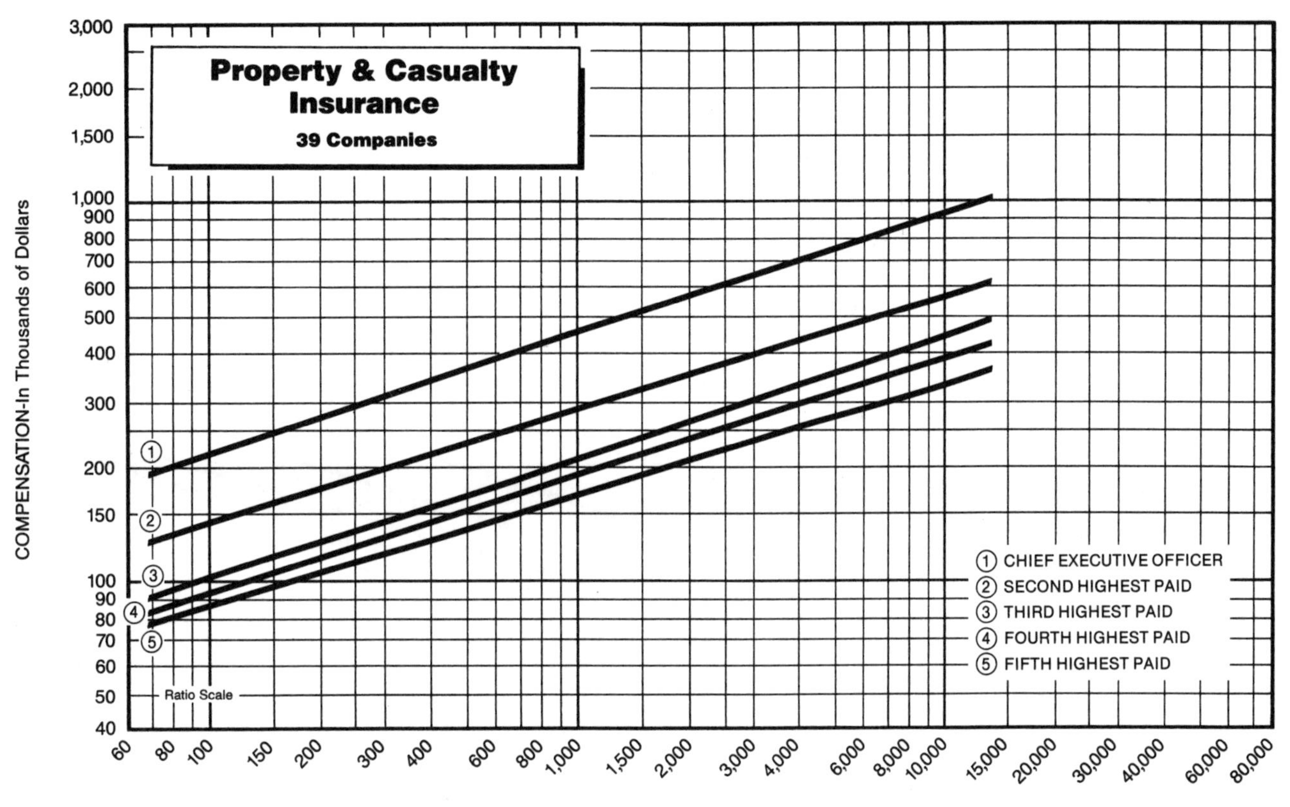

Table 132: 1987 Premium Income

1987 Premium Income	*Companies* Number	Percent
$5 billion and over	6	15%
2-4,999 billion	2	5
1-1,999 billion	4	10
500-999 million	6	15
300-499 million	8	21
200-299 million	3	8
199 million and under	10	26
Total	39	100%

Median	Middle 50% Range Low	High
$445 million	$172 million	$1.5 billion

Table 133: 1987 Total Current Compensation Regression Formula

Compensation Rank	*Formula*	r^2
CEO	log Y = 1.6842 + 0.3236 log X	51%
Second highest	log Y = 1.5530 + 0.3000 log X	43
Third hughest	log Y = 1.3645 + 0.3217 log X	64
Fourth highest	log Y = 1.3394 + 0.3142 log X	64
Fifth highest	log Y = 1.3186 + 0.3031 log X	66

Table 134: 1987 Salary Regression Formula

Compensation Rank	*Formula*	r^2
CEO	log Y = 1.6684 + 0.2794 log X	55%
Second highest	log Y = 1.5261 + 0.2650 log X	45
Third highest	log Y = 1.3545 + 0.2879 log X	57
Fourth highest	log Y = 1.3600 + 0.2711 log X	56
Fifth highest	log Y = 1.3409 + 0.2620 log X	59

Chapter 11
Trade

Chart 17: Total Current Compensation of the Five Highest-Paid Executives, by Company Sales

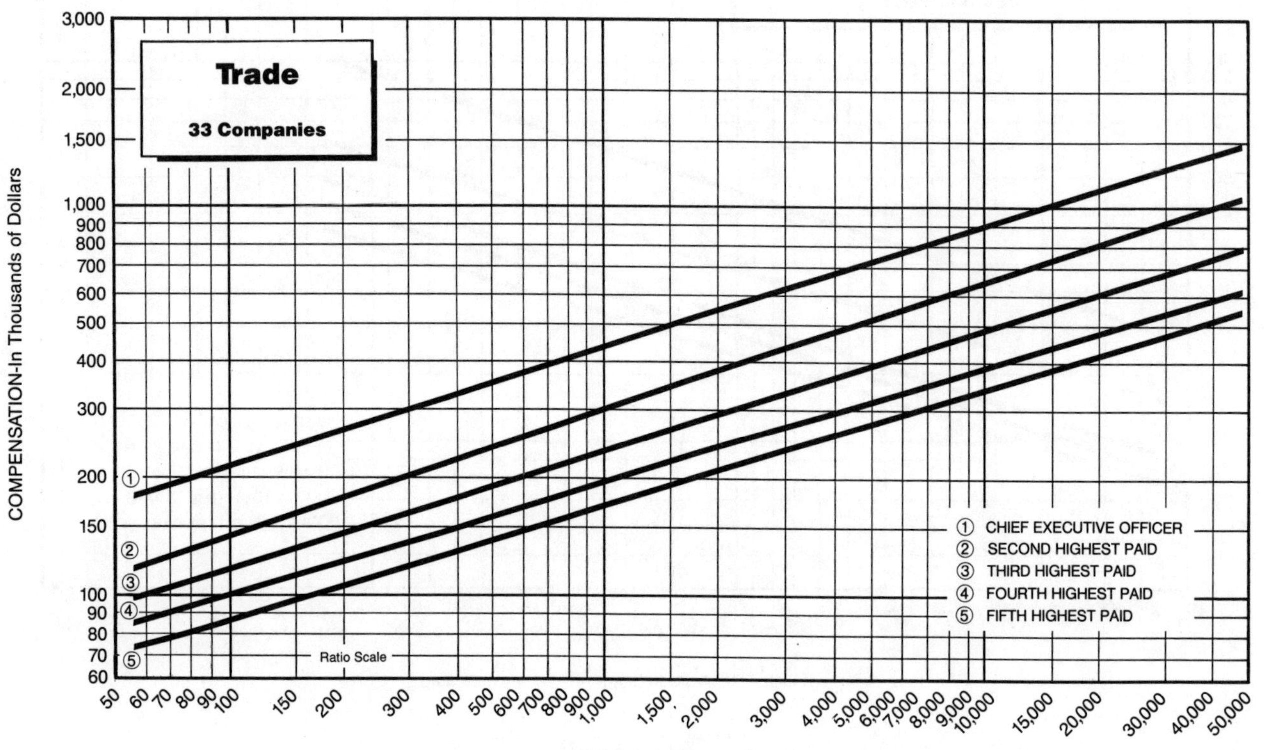

Table 135: 1987 Sales Volume

1987 Sales	*Companies* Number	*Companies* Percent
$5 billion and over	8	24%
2-4,999 billion	4	12
1-1,999 billion	4	12
500-999 million	7	21
300-499 million	6	18
200-299 million	—	—
199 million and under	4	12
Total	33	100%

Median	Middle 50% Range Low	Middle 50% Range High
$971 million	$406 million	$4.2 billion

Table 136: 1987 Total Current Compensation

Compensation Rank	*Median*	*Middle 50% Range* Low	*Middle 50% Range* High
CEO	$413,000	$315,000	$738,000
Second highest	318,000	219,000	566,000
Third highest	268,000	156,000	498,000
Fourth highest	212,000	140,000	298,000
Fifth highest	195,000	120,000	243,000

Table 137: 1987 Total Current Compensation Regression Formula

Compensation Rank	Formula	r^2
CEO	log Y = 1.7318 + 0.3018 log X	69%
Second highest	log Y = 1.4877 + 0.3288 log X	65
Third highest	log Y = 1.4660 + 0.3054 log X	60
Fourth highest	log Y = 1.4235 + 0.2913 log X	68
Fifth highest	log Y = 1.3396 + 0.2982 log X	74

Table 138: Total Current Compensation as a Percentage of CEO's Total Current Compensation

		Middle 50% Range	
Compensation Rank	Median	Low	High
Second highest	70%	58%	82%
Third highest	57	48	65
Fourth highest	46	39	54
Fifth highest	39	32	48

Table 139: 1987 Salary

		Middle 50% Range	
Compensation Rank	Median	Low	High
CEO	$334,000	$250,000	$492,000
Second highest	260,000	165,000	345,000
Third highest	195,000	138,000	344,000
Fourth highest	154,000	126,000	223,000
Fifth highest	140,000	105,000	201,000

Table 140: 1987 Salary Regression Formula

Compensation Rank	Formula	r^2
CEO	log Y = 1.8523 + 0.2222 log X	60%
Second highest	log Y = 1.7175 + 0.2209 log X	50
Third highest	log Y = 1.6169 + 0.2235 log X	51
Fourth highest	log Y = 1.4857 + 0.2397 log X	68
Fifth highest	log Y = 1.4316 + 0.2381 log X	72

Table 141: Salary as a Percentage of CEO's Salary

		Middle 50% Range	
Compensation Rank	Median	Low	High
Second highest	72%	58%	84%
Third highest	58	52	71
Fourth highest	46	40	55
Fifth highest	42	38	49

Table 142: 1987 Bonus Awards (as Percent of Salary), by Company Size

	Sales Volume		
	Middle 50% Range		
Executive	Low $406 Million	Median $971 Million	High $4.2 Billion
CEO			
1987 Bonus	47%	49%	52%
Salary	$242,000	$309,000	$463,000
Second Highest Paid			
1987 Bonus	31%	38%	51%
Salary	$195,000	$238,000	$333,000
Third Highest Paid			
1987 Bonus	26%	32%	43%
Salary	$171,000	$204,000	$274,000
Fourth Highest Paid			
1987 Bonus	29%	32%	38%
Salary	$125,000	$156,000	$227,000
Fifth Highest Paid			
1987 Bonus	27%	30%	37%
Salary	$108,000	$135,000	$196,000

Table 143: 1987 Bonus Awards

1987 Bonus Awards (Percent of Salary)	CEOS		Second Highest Paid		Third Highest Paid		Fourth Highest Paid		Fifth Highest Paid	
	Number	Percent	Number	Percent	Number	Percent	Number	Percent	Number	Percent
100% or more	1	4%	1	4%	—	—	—	—	—	—
75-99	2	8	3	13	2	8%	2	8%	1	4%
60-74	5	21	3	13	3	13	3	13	2	9
50-59	4	17	2	9	2	8	2	8	3	13
40-49	4	17	4	17	7	29	3	13	1	4
30-39	7	29	6	26	6	25	4	17	5	22
Less than 30%	1	4	4	17	4	17	10	42	11	48
Total	24	100%	23	100%	24	100%	24	100%	23	100%
Median Bonus	49%		42%		41%		34%		35%	
Middle 50% Range	34 - 67%		32 - 70%		33 - 50%		22 - 55%		22 - 50%	

Chapter 12
Transportation

Chart 18: Total Current Compensation of the Five Highest-Paid Executives, by Operating Revenue

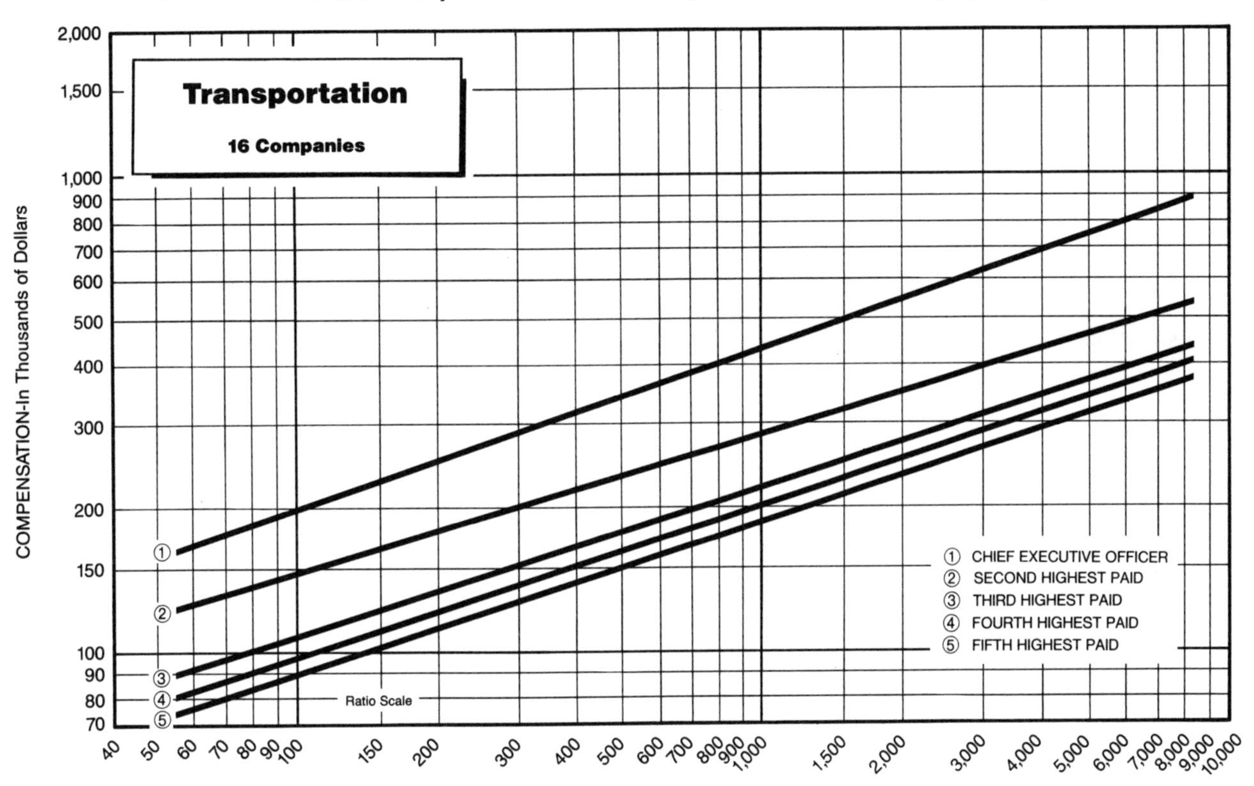

Table 144: 1987 Operating Revenue

1987 Operating Revenue	*Companies* Number	Percent
$5 billion and over	2	13%
2-4,999 billion	2	13
1-1,999 billion	3	19
500-999 million	4	25
300-499 million	2	13
200-299 million	—	—
199 million and under	3	19
Total	16	100%

Median	Middle 50% Range	
	Low	High
$632 million	$346 million	$1.9 billion

Table 145: 1987 Total Current Compensation

Compensation Rank	*Median*	*Middle 50% Range*	
		Low	*High*
CEO	$355,000	$265,000	$693,000
Second highest	233,000	200,000	360,000
Third highest	156,000	139,000	289,000
Fourth highest	150,000	125,000	256,000
Fifth highest	146,000	110,000	230,000

Table 146: 1987 Total Current Compensation Regression Formula

Compensation Rank	Formula	r^2
CEO	$\log Y = 1.6132 + 0.3416 \log X$	60%
Second highest	$\log Y = 1.5531 + 0.3028 \log X$	57
Third highest	$\log Y = 1.4072 + 0.3162 \log X$	61
Fourth highest	$\log Y = 1.3352 + 0.3245 \log X$	69
Fifth highest	$\log Y = 1.2948 + 0.3250 \log X$	73

Table 147: Total Current Compensation as a Percentage of CEO's Total Current Compensation

		Middle 50% Range	
Compensation Rank	Median	Low	High
Second highest	64%	56%	85%
Third highest	51	42	57
Fourth highest	48	40	55
Fifth highest	42	36	49

Table 148: 1987 Salary

		Middle 50% Range	
Compensation Rank	Median	Low	High
CEO	$265,000	$190,000	$466,000
Second highest	225,000	136,000	250,000
Third highest	150,000	100,000	206,000
Fourth highest	113,000	93,000	200,000
Fifth highest	108,000	90,000	200,000

Table 149: 1987 Salary Regression Formula

Compensation Rank	Formula	r^2
CEO	$\log Y = 1.7202 + 0.2503 \log X$	39%
Second highest	$\log Y = 1.6879 + 0.2059 \log X$	36
Third highest	$\log Y = 1.5016 + 0.2361 \log X$	52
Fourth highest	$\log Y = 1.4037 + 0.2563 \log X$	63
Fifth highest	$\log Y = 1.3799 + 0.2530 \log X$	67

Table 150: Salary as a Percentage of CEO's Salary

		Middle 50% Range	
Compensation Rank	Median	Low	High
Second highest	63%	57%	83%
Third highest	51	44	60
Fourth highest	47	44	57
Fifth highest	45	42	56

Chapter 13

Utilities

Chart 19: Total Current Compensation of the Five Highest-Paid Executives, by Operating Revenue

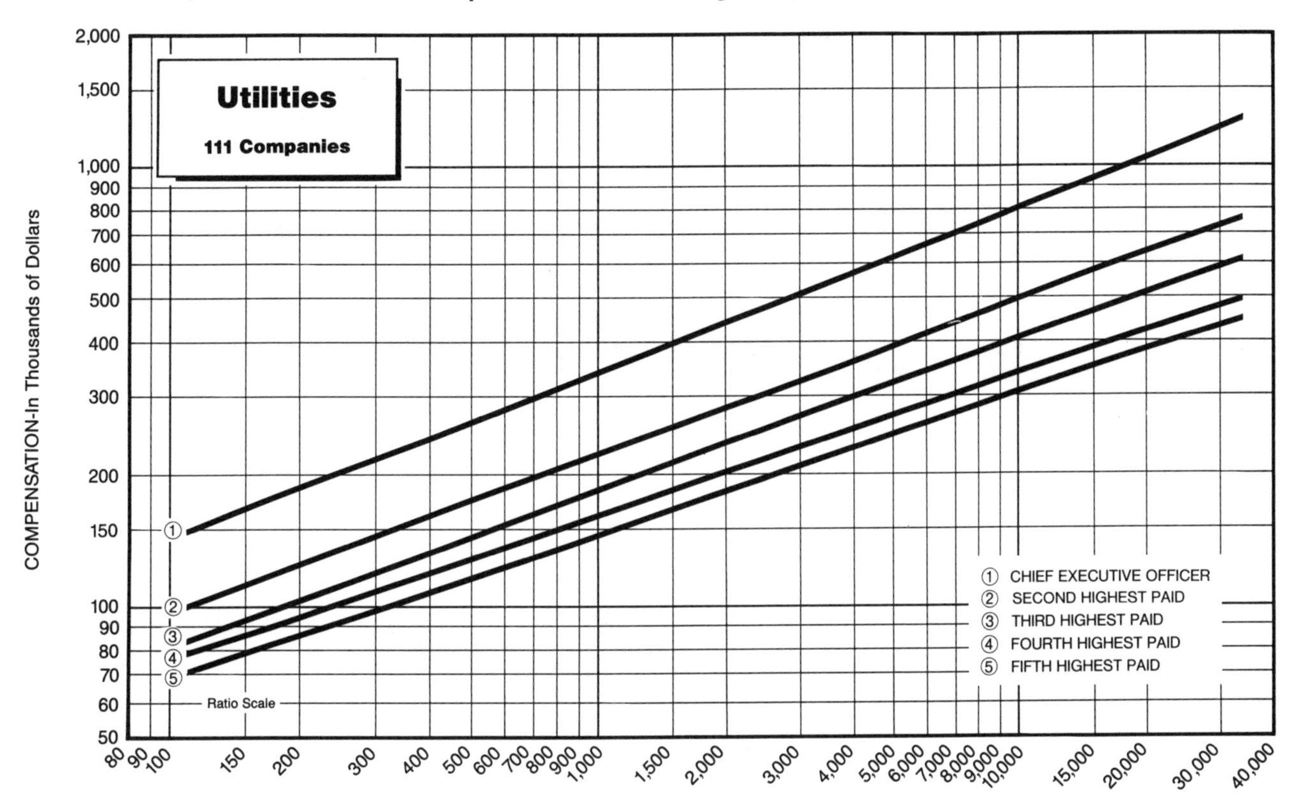

Table 151: 1987 Operating Revenue

1987 Operating Revenue	*Companies*	
	Number	*Percent*
$5 billion and over	11	10%
2-4,999 billion	18	16
1-1,999 billion	28	25
500-999 million	18	16
300-499 million	14	13
200-299 million	5	5
199 million and under	17	15
Total	111	100%

Median	Middle 50% Range	
	Low	High
$1.1 billion	$361 million	$2.1 billion

Table 152: 1987 Total Current Compensation

Compensation Rank	*Median*	*Middle 50% Range*	
		Low	*High*
CEO	$355,000	$223,000	$489,000
Second highest	218,000	155,000	315,000
Third highest	171,000	118,000	253,000
Fourth highest	149,000	105,000	214,000
Fifth highest	142,000	103,000	185,000

Table 153: 1987 Total Current Compensation Regression Formula

Compensation Rank	Formula	r^2
CEO	$\log Y = 1.4031 + 0.3770 \log X$	64%
Second highest	$\log Y = 1.2800 + 0.3554 \log X$	65
Third highest	$\log Y = 1.2006 + 0.3528 \log X$	68
Fourth highest	$\log Y = 1.2094 + 0.3330 \log X$	66
Fifth highest	$\log Y = 1.1853 + 0.3258 \log X$	71

Table 154: Total Current Compensation as a Percentage of CEO's Total Current Compensation

		Middle 50% Range	
Compensation Rank	Median	Low	High
Second highest	66%	58%	74%
Third highest	53	48	59
Fourth highest	48	42	54
Fifth highest	43	38	48

Table 155: 1987 Salary

		Middle 50% Range	
Compensation Rank	Median	Low	High
CEO	$290,000	$198,000	$410,000
Second highest	185,000	141,000	275,000
Third highest	157,000	110,000	217,000
Fourth highest	143,000	103,000	184,000
Fifth highest	128,000	96,000	161,000

Table 156: 1987 Salary Regression Formula

Compensation Rank	Formula	r^2
CEO	$\log Y = 1.5269 + 0.3111 \log X$	63%
Second highest	$\log Y = 1.4206 + 0.2863 \log X$	65
Third highest	$\log Y = 1.3492 + 0.2827 \log X$	66
Fourth highest	$\log Y = 1.3297 + 0.2740 \log X$	67
Fifth highest	$\log Y = 1.2954 + 0.2725 \log X$	70

Table 157: Salary as a Percentage of CEO's Salary

		Middle 50% Range	
Compensation Rank	Median	Low	High
Second highest	67%	59%	74%
Third highest	55	50	60
Fourth highest	49	43	54
Fifth highest	44	40	50

Table 158: 1987 Bonus Awards (as Percent of Salary), by Company Size

	Operating Revenue		
	Middle 50% Range		
Executive	Low $361 Million	Median $1.1 Billion	High $2.1 Billion
CEO			
1987 Bonus	23%	33%	40%
Salary	$226,000	$312,000	$376,000
Second Highest Paid			
1987 Bonus	20%	30%	37%
Salary	$149,000	$202,000	$241,000
Third Highest Paid			
1987 Bonus	15%	26%	33%
Salary	$126,000	$170,000	$201,000
Fourth Highest Paid			
1987 Bonus	15%	24%	30%
Salary	$112,000	$152,000	$181,000
Fifth Highest Paid			
1987 Bonus	14%	22%	26%
Salary	$ 99,800	$136,000	$163,000

Table 159: 1987 Bonus Awards

1987 Bonus Awards (Percent of Salary)	CEOS		Second Highest Paid		Third Highest Paid		Fourth Highest Paid		Fifth Highest Paid	
	Number	Percent	Number	Percent	Number	Percent	Number	Percent	Number	Percent
100% or more	1	2%	1	2%	3	5%	—	—	—	—
90-99	2	3	1	2	—	—	—	—	1	2%
80-89	1	2	2	3	—	—	—	—	+	+
70-79	1	2	1	2	—	—	3	5%	—	—
60-69	5	9	2	3	3	5	1	2	2	4
50-59	8	14	5	9	3	5	5	9	2	4
40-49	3	5	6	10	5	9	7	12	6	11
30-39	13	22	12	20	13	23	8	14	10	18
20-29	7	12	8	14	9	16	10	18	9	16
10-19	14	24	17	29	13	23	17	30	20	35
Less than 10%	3	5	4	7	7	13	6	11	7	12
Total	58	100%	59	100%	56	100%	57	100%	57	100%
Median Bonus	31%		30%		27%		24%		23%	
Middle 50% Range	18 - 53%		17 - 45%		15 - 37%		14 - 42%		13 - 33%	

Appendix

Procedure for Using Regression Equations

In the equations, X is sales volume, total deposits (commercial banking), premium income (insurance), or operating revenue (transportation and utilities). These are expressed in millions of dollars. That is, six zeroes are dropped. Y is total current compensation or salary expressed in thousands of dollars. That is, three zeroes are dropped. The "coefficient of determination" (r^2) is given in each formula. This is the ratio of the variation in total current compensation or salary explained by the regression line to the total variation in pay. (The square root of this coefficient is the correlation coefficient.) The logarithms are base ten.

Example:

Using the equation log Y = 1.7390 + 0.3000 (log X), one can calculate the total current compensation of the chief executive in a company with sales of $500 million.

1. First set X = 500, that is, 500,000,000 with six zeroes dropped.
2. Log X = 2.6990
3. Multiply log X by 0.3000, which is the coefficient of the variable log X in the given equation. This results in a value of 0.8097.
4. Add to 0.8097 the constant in the equation, 1.7390. The result, 2.5487, is the value of log Y.
5. The chief executive's total current compensation is the antilog of log Y, which is 354. Read in thousands of dollars it is $354,000.

Equation: log Y = 1.7390 + 0.3000 (log X)
X = $500,000,000 = 500
log X = 2.6990
log Y = 1.7390 + 0.3000 (2.6990)
log Y = 1.7390 + 0.8097
log Y = 2.5487
antilog Y = 354
Y = $354,000